W9-BAO-433

More than
170 heirloom recipes
for remembered tastes
and cherished traditions

 Also by Lois Wyse

Funny, You Don't Look Like a Grandmother

Grandchildren Are So Much Fun,
I Should Have Had Them First

You Wouldn't Believe What
My Grandchild Did

Women Make the Best Friends

Friend to Friend

Just Like Grandma Used to Make...

Lois Wyse

with

Liza Antelo and Sherri Pincus

Simon & Schuster

SIMON & SCHUSTER
Rockefeller Center
1230 Avenue of the Americas
New York, NY 10020

Copyright © 1998 by Garret Press
All rights reserved,
including the right of reproduction
in whole or in part in any form.

SIMON & SCHUSTER and colophon are registered trademarks
of Simon & Schuster Inc.

BOOK DESIGNED BY DEBORAH KERNER

Manufactured in the United States of America
1   3   5   7   9   10   8   6   4   2
Library of Congress Cataloging-in-Publication Data
Wyse, Lois
Just like grandma used to make / Lois Wyse, with Liza Antelo and Sherri Pincus.
p.   cm.
Includes index.
I. Cookery, International.   I. Antelo, Liza.   II. Pincus, Sherri.   III. Title
TX725.A1W97   1998
641.59—dc21   97-44173
CIP

ISBN 0-684-82686-0

ACKNOWLEDGMENTS

Recipe books, like recipes themselves, are best when several cooks have input. We are grateful to many of our favorite cooks for adding the touches to make this book worthy of the recipes it recalls.

We thank our editor Sydny Miner, who gave us significant guidelines and encouragement, and was helpful throughout our work. We are grateful beyond measure to the named and unnamed friends, relatives, and acquaintances who shared their family treasures, these recipes. We regret that space prevented us from including even more of the superb recipe and food ideas we were offered.

Liza thanks her husband, Joe Antelo, for the Spanish touches in some recipes; Sherri is grateful to her husband Ted for lending not only moral support but the use of office space and computers. And both of them thank their husbands for tasting and trying the recipes along with them.

Lois is grateful to her mother for recalling family favorites and to her children, Katherine and Robert, who often use Nana's recipes and teach them to their children.

For the mothers

and grandmothers who

showed us the way to the kitchen

and to life

STANDARD WEIGHTS AND MEASURES

Make certain all measurements are level.

Dash	= 8 drops
1 tablespoon	= 3 teaspoons
4 tablespoons	= ¼ cup
5⅓ tablespoons	= ⅓ cup
8 tablespoons	= ½ cup
16 tablespoons	= 1 cup (dry)
1 fluid ounce	= 2 tablespoons
1 cup (liquid)	= ½ pint
2 cups (16 ounces)	= 1 pint
2 pints (4 cups)	= 1 quart
4 quarts	= 1 gallon
8 quarts	= 1 peck (dry)
4 pecks	= 1 bushel
16 ounces (dry measure)	= 1 pound

Other Measurements

1 lemon	= 2–3 tablespoons juice and 2 teaspoons zest
1 orange	= 6–8 tablespoons juice and 2–3 tablespoons zest
1 cup heavy cream	= 2 cups whipped cream
2 cups water	= 1 pound
5 large whole eggs 6 medium 7 small	= 1 cup, approximately

8 large egg whites
10–11 medium } = 1 cup, approximately
11–12 small

12 large egg yolks
13–14 medium } = 1 cup, approximately
15–16 small

Fluid Measure Equivalents

METRIC	UNITED STATES	BRITISH
1 liter	4½ cups *or* 1 quart 2 ounces	1¾ pints
1 demiliter (½ liter)	2 cups (generous) *or* 1 pint (generous)	¾ pint (generous)
1 deciliter (⅒ liter)	½ cup (scant) *or* ¼ pint (scant)	3–4 ounces

Measure Equivalents

METRIC	UNITED STATES	BRITISH
1.00 gram	.035 ounce	.035 ounce
28.35 grams	1 ounce	1 ounce
100.00 grams	3.5 ounces	3.5 ounces
114.00 grams	4 ounces (approximately)	4 ounces (approximately)
226.78 grams	8 ounces	8 ounces
500.00 grams	1 pound 1.5 ounces	1 pound 1.5 ounces
1.00 kilogram	2.21 pounds	2.21 pounds

Comparative U.S., British and Metric Weights and Measures
for Ingredients Important to Pastry Makers

INGREDIENT	UNITED STATES	BRITISH	METRIC
Almond paste	1¾ cups	16 ounces	450 grams
Apples, pared/sliced	1 cup	4 ounces	125 grams
Berries	1¾ cups	6 ounces	190 grams
Butter	1 tablespoon	½ ounce	15 grams
	½ cup	4 ounces	125 grams
	2 cups	1 pound (generous)	450 grams
Cheese	1 pound (generous)	1 pound (generous)	450 grams
Cheese, grated hard type	1 cup (scant)	4 ounces (scant)	100 grams
Cheese, cottage	1 cup	16 ounces	450 grams
Cheese, cream	6 tablespoons	3 ounces	80 grams
Cornstarch	1 tablespoon	⅓ ounce	10 grams
Flour	¼ cup	1¼ ounces	35 grams
(unsifted)	½ cup	2½ ounces	70 grams
	1 cup	4¾ ounces	142 grams
	3½ cups	1 pound	450 grams
Herbs, fresh/chopped	1 tablespoon	½ ounce	15 grams
Nuts, chopped	1 cup	5½ ounces	155 grams
Raisins	1 tablespoon	⅓ ounce	10 grams
(seedless)	1 cup	5⅓ ounces	160 grams
	3 cups	1 pound	450 grams
Spices, ground	1 teaspoon	⅟₁₂ ounce	2.5 grams
	2 tablespoons	½ ounce	15 grams
Sugar,	1 teaspoon	⅙ ounce	5 grams
granulated	1 tablespoon	½ ounce	15 grams
	¼ cup	2 ounces	60 grams
	1 cup	8 ounces	226 grams

INGREDIENT	UNITED STATES	BRITISH	METRIC
Sugar, confectioners'	¼ cup	I ounce (generous)	35 grams
	½ cup	2¼ ounces (scant)	70 grams
	I cup	4½ ounces (scant)	140 grams
Sugar, brown	I tablespoon	⅓ ounce	10 grams
	½ cup	2⅔ ounces	80 grams
	I cup	5⅓ ounces	160 grams

CONTENTS

Just Like Grandma Used to Make...

INTRODUCTION

IT WAS A FEW DAYS BEFORE THANKSGIVING, AND MY MOTHER CALLED TO SAY WHAT SHE SAYS EVERY YEAR, "I'LL MAKE NUT CUPS AND THE POPPY-SEED PASTRIES YOU LOVE."

Maybe pumpkin pie and bread pudding make your turkey trot, but in my house if we don't serve Nana's nut cups, it isn't a holiday.

It was when I began setting the table that I first realized that the heritage of the women in my family is not diamonds and rubies. It is poppy seed and chocolate. It is the recipe for turkey dressing borrowed from a friend's grandmother, and sweet potatoes made the way a neighbor showed me. In other homes it is marinara sauce and Grandma's cookies, for in all our families we treasure recipes from generation to generation as if they were the gold chains of the Empress. Food is the traditional gift of mothers to daughters (and sons). Only the recipes change. One family's inheritance of Greek pastries is another's hush puppies. Our universal patrimony is made of tastes and smells: French coq au vin, Hungarian paprikash, Swedish meatballs, New Orleans shrimp gumbo.

Unfortunately, like the histories of many of our families, our history of traditional foods often goes unrecorded. No one bothers to write the menu or document the recipes.

Our grandmothers often failed to realize (and so did many of us) that what we most wanted Grandmother to hand down to us were her recipes, Grandmother food the way Grandmother made it. But who of our grandmothers was precise when it came to measuring? Grandmother made foods by feel and taste ("roll the dough until it feels good"), thought little about amounts ("and put in some sugar"). Some of our grandmothers, of course, came from countries and times when the girl in the family was not the one taught to read and write.

So, since grandmothers often failed to leave their recipes, many of us have tried to follow our noses and remember the fragrance of cookies and cakes baking in the old oven; or we roll the tape of memory and play back the picture of Grandmother in her kitchen and try to watch as she made those foods we can still taste.

Even when grandmothers did let us follow them around the kitchen, they were not always forthcoming. Michael Tilson Thomas remembers asking, "Grandmother, how do you make strudel?" And Grandmother answered, "First you pin up your hair. Then you put on a clean apron. Then you wash your hands. Then you make the strudel."

Yet even when we know the recipes, we sometimes have trouble getting "the grandma touch." Sharon Miller recalls her Polish grandmother, who made her strudel with lard instead of butter. "The sheets were absolutely transparent after she rolled them. It all came out so flaky, so perfect when she did it. Her daughters and granddaughters could never duplicate it. My mother came close, but even she didn't quite get it. After I married, I kept telling Grandma I was trying, but I never succeeded.

"And then one day, in my kitchen, I started making Grandma's strudel. I'm not sure just how I changed things, but that day when the strudel came from the oven, it looked just like hers. And when I tasted it, I knew I had it! I couldn't wait to tell Grandma. At that very minute the telephone rang, and my cousin called to tell me that our grandmother had just died. Of course we were sad, but I like to think that Grandma waited—she'd been ill a long time—until I made the perfect strudel, and then she knew she could go in peace."

What is it that gives grandmother food its special taste? Certainly love plays a part, but so does a sure touch. We complain because Grandmother never tells us *exactly* how much salt to add to the stroganoff or because Grandmother's recipe for stuffed peppers doesn't specify the amount of rice. What we forget is that our grandmothers made their foods by heart and by touch and with a kind of familiarity that came with the territory. Not only had they watched their mothers, but they knew their food from the ground up. The children grew up in the country where they picked the tomatoes and beans, the corn and greens they had planted. They helped raise the cows and pigs and chickens that were slaughtered for the family table, so that when it came to freshness and quality, they knew what to expect. Today we are not certain whether the greenhouse tomatoes will have the same taste as the Jersey tomatoes, so we follow recipes to make our fresh tomato sauce and wonder: Do different varieties of certain foods need more of a boost? More herbs? More pepper? A touch of salt?

We worry that we cannot follow recipes to the letter, yet cookbooks (yes, even this one) are not written with the idea that anyone will follow the directions slavishly. We hope that you will consider this book a road map—it will show you how to get from the kitchen

Lois Wyse

to the table, but we want you to try a few side roads, too. Experiment with your garden or the garden the supermarket offers. Trust your own judgment. Test your creativity and, if it doesn't work, there's always next time.

Use herbs and garnishes, those accessories in your cooking. After all, we all wear black dresses, yet we don't all look the same. We can all make meatloaf—but just think of the variations as we mix and match different ingredients.

What we have tried to do in this cookbook is to gather the recipes of remembered tastes and lives. There are surefire American recipes that come from the days when the world had front porches, and Mom's apple pie was a staple in the kitchen, not a joke in a comedy club. There are recipes from Europe, the Middle East, the Far East, and Central and South America because those are places where so many of our recipes were first made. This book has been a loving collaboration with dear friends Liza Antelo and Sherri Pincus, who collected and tested the recipes. In making and testing our recipes even our old friendship deepened, because there is no place like the kitchen for sharing secrets—and recipes.

All three of us hope that this book will inspire you to look in your own family recipe books, ask within your own family circle, and uncover the long-hidden treasure, the legacy of your own grandmothers.

A P P E T I Z E R S

"Eat, darling, eat."

REMEMBER HOW HUNGRY YOU WERE WHEN YOU WENT TO GRANDMOTHER'S?

WAS IT THE ANTICIPATION OF THE FAMILY GET-TOGETHER?

Was it because you always arrived just a touch underfed so you could eat and eat and eat?

After all, Grandmother's portions were never sparing, and the highest compliment one could pay a grandmother was to ask for seconds.

Grandmother may have eschewed the cocktail hour, but no granny worth her wooden spoon ever let a grandchild go hungry waiting for the main event. Instead there were appetizers ("a little something to eat until we eat"), often served with tomato juice at the table or in the seldom-used living room where everyone had to be careful not to mess the antimacassars.

APPETIZERS

Sesame Cheese Wafers

Hummus Dip

Chopped Liver

Swedish Meatballs

Dolmas

Empanadas

Cheese Boureks

Potato Cheese Pierogi

Hot Bacon-Horseradish Dip

Sesame Cheese Wafers

Seranna knew her grandmother didn't invent sesame seeds, but she used them every time she could. "I suppose it was a matter of texture and flavor," Seranna said. "Oh, how I loved the feel and the crunch when I bit into her sesame cheese wafers."

MAKES 80 TO 90 WAFERS

1 cup all-purpose flour
1 teaspoon salt
5 tablespoons butter, softened, plus
    additional for greasing pan.
1 cup grated cheddar cheese
¼ cup sesame seeds, lightly
    toasted

¼ teaspoon ground white
    pepper or cayenne
    pepper
dash Worcestershire sauce
2–3 tablespoons ice water

Preheat oven to 400 degrees.

Grease a cookie sheet. In a medium bowl, combine the flour, salt, butter, cheese, sesame seeds, pepper, and Worcestershire sauce and mix well. Add ice water, I tablespoon at a time, and work into a smooth dough. Divide the dough into two I- x 8-inch rolls. Chill for I hour.

To bake wafers, slice rolls into thin slices, about ⅛-inch thick. Place wafers on prepared cookie sheet and prick tops with a fork. Bake for about 10 to 12 minutes, until crisp and light golden brown. Serve warm.

NOTE: *To toast sesame seeds, preheat oven to 300 degrees. Spread seeds out on small cookie sheet. Toast 6–8 minutes. Watch carefully.*

Hummus Dip

aisie could tell how she would spend an hour when her Lebanese grandmother was making hummus, because once the chickpeas were put up to boil and softened, Maisie knew it would be her job to peel carefully each outer skin. And, although this is not included in our recipe, Maisie remembers that her grandmother always drizzled olive oil (generously, of course—we're talking about grandmothers) over the hummus until it fairly swam with good taste!

MAKES 2 CUPS

1 pound dried chickpeas, soaked
    overnight in cold water to cover
2–3 cloves garlic, minced
2 fresh lemons, juiced
⅓ cup sesame paste (tahini)

2–3 tablespoons olive oil
1 tablespoon chopped fresh parsley
1 tablespoon chopped fresh chives
dash paprika

Drain peas, rinse, and put in deep pot. Pour in boiling water to cover, simmer over low heat about 30 minutes. Drain again. Put back in pot, cover with cold water and cook over low heat another 2 hours, or until very tender. Drain well.

Put cooked peas in processor or food mill and puree until smooth. Add garlic, lemon juice, tahini, and oil and puree or mix well. If mixture seems too thick or dry, add a bit more oil or water. It should have the consistency of mayonnaise. Stir in herbs and transfer to serving bowl. Dust top with paprika and serve with pita bread or crackers.

NOTE: *If dried chickpeas are not available, use 2 cups canned chickpeas, also called garbanzos, well rinsed and drained.*

Lois Wyse

Chopped Liver

ubbie Becky's chopped liver is spread over every memory of her family dinners, but no Jewish grandmother worth her chicken soup ever failed to make chopped liver part of Friday night Shabbat dinner. Indeed, once the candles were lit and the blessings said, the children were always sure to ask, "Now can we have chopped liver?"

MAKES 2 CUPS

1 pound fresh chicken livers	*1 large onion, diced*
1–2 slices fresh calf's liver (about ½ pound)	*4 hard-cooked eggs*
	½ teaspoon salt
1–2 tablespoons rendered chicken fat (recipe follows)	*freshly ground black pepper to taste*

Carefully look over chicken livers, removing any green spots or cartilage. Check calf's liver for casing along edges and remove.

Cut calf's liver into small pieces. Heat 1 tablespoon of fat in skillet and sauté onions and livers over medium heat 8–10 minutes, or until golden brown. The livers should be firm and cooked through. Remove from heat and cool mixture to room temperature. When cool, run the liver, onions, and eggs, through a meat grinder or a food processor. Be careful not to puree the mixture. Add any juices left in skillet and season mixture with salt and pepper. Add additional fat as needed. The mixture should be moist and of spreading consistency.

Chopped liver is best served shortly after it is made. Serve on crackers or a lettuce leaf with a sprinkle of chopped fresh parsley.

To render CHICKEN FAT:

1 cup or more solid pieces of chicken fat, pulled from fresh chickens	*1 large onion, diced*

Put ingredients into deep saucepan along with any pieces of skin attached to the fat. Cook slowly, uncovered, over low heat, until fat melts. Continue to cook about 45 minutes, or until onions have turned a rich amber brown, and any skin in the pot looks very brown and crisp. Cool.

Strain through a fine mesh strainer, pressing on solids to extract liquid fat. Discard solids, and store fat, refrigerated, in airtight container.

Swedish Meatballs

In collecting recipes we not only asked grandmothers, we talked to grandfathers. Liza asked her own father (now a great-grandfather) what he remembered about his Finnish childhood, and his answer was "meatballs." Meatballs were sometimes a main course, often an appetizer, in many European countries. Whether your grandmother served "Swedish meatballs," "Hungarian meatballs," or "Italian meatballs," they are still meat with spices.

So, where's the difference?

In the spicing—and that's the reason Italian meatballs will never taste like the ones Liza's father remembers.

MAKES 6 TO 8 SERVINGS

6 tablespoons butter, divided
1 medium onion, finely chopped
½ pound each ground beef, veal, and/or
    pork, mixed together
½ cup fresh bread crumbs
½ cup milk or cream
2 eggs, lightly beaten
¼ teaspoon ground nutmeg
¼ teaspoon ground allspice
1 teaspoon salt, or to taste

½ teaspoon ground white pepper
2 tablespoons all-purpose flour
2 cups rich beef or chicken stock, or a
    mixture
1 teaspoon Worcestershire sauce
2–3 tablespoons sour cream, optional
1 teaspoon snipped fresh dill
1 teaspoon chopped fresh parsley, for
    garnish

Lois Wyse

In a skillet, melt 2 tablespoons butter and sauté onions until soft and golden.

Put onions in bowl and add meat. Mix in bread crumbs and milk. Add eggs, nutmeg, allspice, salt, and pepper. Knead mixture for a few minutes. Chill 30 minutes.

Wet hands and shape meat into small balls. Place meatballs on cookie sheet and chill 30 minutes.

Heat 1 tablespoon butter at a time in a heavy skillet, and fry meatballs over medium heat about 5 minutes, or until golden brown. Fry in batches and do not overcrowd pan. Add more butter as necessary until all meatballs have been cooked. Set aside.

Stir flour into remaining butter in pan and whisk to form a *roux,* or paste. Whisk in stock and bring to boil. Cook a few minutes. Add Worcestershire sauce, remove from heat, and whisk in sour cream and dill. Add meatballs to the sauce and heat through. Do not let sauce boil, or sour cream will curdle. Garnish with parsley, if desired. Serve in a chafing dish along with toothpicks.

Dolmas

Alleta grew up in Greece, and remembers picking grape leaves and helping her mother and grandmother soak them in brine—for that was the little girl's role in making dolmas.

MAKES 3 DOZEN DOLMAS

1–2 tablespoons olive oil
1 medium onion, finely chopped
1 clove garlic, minced
¼ cup long-grain rice
2 tablespoons pine nuts
1 tablespoon chopped seedless raisins
½ pound ground beef
½ pound ground lamb
1 teaspoon salt
1 teaspoon dried mint flakes, or 1
	tablespoon chopped fresh mint

1 tablespoon chopped fresh flat-leaf
	parsley
1 teaspoon grated fresh lemon rind
½ teaspoon freshly ground black pepper
½ teaspoon dried oregano
¼ teaspoon ground cinnamon
1 one-pound jar grape leaves, well rinsed
1½ cups boiling water, chicken stock, or
	tomato juice, or a mixture
1 tablespoon honey
¼ cup fresh lemon juice

Over medium heat, heat oil in skillet, and sauté onion, garlic, rice, pine nuts and raisins 2–3 minutes, until softened. Transfer to a bowl, cool and mix in meat, salt, mint, parsley, lemon rind, pepper, oregano, and cinnamon.

Place a vine leaf on a board, *vein-side up*. Place a tablespoon of filling in the center, fold over sides, and roll into a cylinder. Do not roll too tightly, as rice needs room for expansion. Continue until all the filling has been used.

Cover the bottom of a large shallow pan with all leftover vine leaves and pieces. Place dolmas in neat rows along the bottom of the pan, seam-side down, and fairly close together so they fit snugly. If there are more than will fill one layer, start a second layer. Mix the liquid, honey, and lemon juice together and pour over dolmas. Place a glass pie plate over dolmas to weigh them down and help keep their shape while cooking.

Cover the pan, and simmer 30–40 minutes, until rice has absorbed most of the liquid. Remove pie plate.

Cool to room temperature. Drain off excess liquid and serve garnished with lemon slices.

Lois Wyse

Empanadas

Empanadas are not exactly the eggs and bacon of Spain, but Rosita recalls them as the hallmark dish of the best cook in the family. Empanadas can be served as an afterschool snack or main dish, as well as an appetizer. In each Spanish family there is one cook whose name brings forth sighs followed by, "Now *there* was an empanada maker."

MAKES APPROXIMATELY 4 DOZEN

DOUGH

1½ cups all-purpose flour

1 teaspoon salt

¼ teaspoon paprika

6 tablespoons butter, chilled

2 tablespoons vegetable shortening

1–2 tablespoons ice water

Combine flour, salt, and paprika in a large mixing bowl. Using fingertips, work in butter a few bits at a time, then shortening. Continue working until mixture resembles fine grains of sand. Add water, one tablespoon at a time, until mixture comes together and forms a soft ball. Turn out onto flat, floured surface and knead with heel of hand for a few minutes until completely smooth. Gather dough, wrap in plastic wrap, and refrigerate.

Prepare FILLING:

1–2 tablespoons olive oil

½ pound ground lamb or beef

1 small onion, minced

1 clove of garlic, minced

2 tablespoons dried currants

2 tablespoons tomato paste

2 tablespoons chopped fresh parsley

1 tablespoon capers, drained

1 hard-cooked egg, finely chopped

¼ cup pimento-stuffed green olives, finely chopped

salt and freshly ground pepper, to taste

Pinch of cayenne pepper

¼ teaspoon ground cumin

¼ teaspoon ground coriander

1 egg, beaten with 1 tablespoon cold water

In a large skillet, heat oil and sauté meat with onion. Use a fork to break up chunks of meat. Cook over medium heat about 5 minutes. Add garlic, currants, tomato paste, parsley, and ca-

continued on next page

pers and cook another 2 minutes. Stir in the egg, olives, salt, pepper, cayenne, cumin, and coriander and continue cooking, another 2 minutes. Transfer to a bowl to cool. Make sure mixture is finely ground with no large pieces remaining.

Preheat oven to 350 degrees. Grease cookie sheets and a 3-inch cookie cutter.

Roll out chilled dough to ⅛-inch thickness and cut out rounds. Brush each round with egg wash, put a heaping teaspoon of filling in the center, and fold over dough to create a crescent shape. Press ends of dough together with tines of a fork. Brush tops of patties with remaining egg wash. Transfer *empanadas* to cookie sheet.

Bake 20 minutes, or until crisp and golden.

Cheese Boureks

reek and Sephardic grandmothers always had a good hand with *boureks*. They seemed almost "to the phyllo born." Our Greek friend, Ana, remembers moving into her first apartment and inviting her parents and grandmother to dinner for her first try at a home-cooked all-Greek meal. She bought a package of phyllo and proceeded to roll and roll while the phyllo got tougher and tougher. Finally she admitted to herself that she just didn't have the family's phyllo fingers, gave up, and went to the corner grocery for crescent rolls.

MAKES 28 BOUREKS

1 pound farmer or pot cheese
8 ounces feta cheese, diced
2 tablespoons butter
2 large leeks, whites only, chopped
1 tablespoon fresh dill, chopped
salt and freshly ground black pepper to
    taste

1 whole egg and 1 egg yolk
1 one-pound package phyllo dough,
    defrosted
1 pound butter, melted

Preheat oven to 400 degrees. Grease a cookie sheet.

Put cheeses into bowl. Heat 2 tablespoons butter in a small skillet, and sauté leeks for a few minutes until soft. Stir into cheeses with dill and salt and pepper to taste. Add eggs and mix well.

Unfold phyllo dough onto flat surface. Cover with a damp towel to prevent drying. Lift one sheet of dough onto a board and brush surface with melted butter. Continue brushing and stacking with five more sheets for a total of six layers. Cut dough into four quarters and put a heaping tablespoon of the filling in the center of each quarter. Flatten mixture slightly and fold dough up and over filling. Tuck sides under to create a small rectangle of pastry. Repeat this process until all dough and filling has been used.

Transfer *boureks* to ungreased cookie sheet. Brush tops with additional melted butter. Bake *boureks* for about 20 minutes, or until golden brown, crisp, and puffy.

Potato Cheese Pierogi

Lucina admits that she rarely takes the time to make pierogi now that she can buy them in the specialty-food section of the supermarket. "But on days when I want to prove that, even though I have a top engineering job, I can still cook like a grandma, I go in the kitchen for my own 'r and r.'"

MAKES 4 TO 5 DOZEN PIEROGI

FILLING:

4 large Idaho potatoes, peeled and cut
   into chunks
6 tablespoons unsalted butter
1 small onion, finely chopped

½ pound farmer or pot cheese
½ teaspoon salt
¼ teaspoon freshly ground black pepper

DOUGH:

4 cups all-purpose flour
½ teaspoon salt
2 tablespoons unsalted butter, melted

1 whole egg and 1 egg yolk
2 cups lukewarm water

SUGGESTED GARNISHES:

Melted butter
chopped fresh parsley
crumbled bacon

sour cream
fresh applesauce

Boil potatoes in lightly salted water until tender, about 20 minutes. Drain well and set aside.

Melt butter in small skillet and sauté onion slowly over low heat until soft and golden brown, about 15 minutes.

Grind potatoes and cheese together through a meat grinder or ricer. Add onion mixture to potatoes, along with salt and pepper. Mix well.

PREPARE DOUGH:

Sift flour with salt onto a flat surface and make a well in the center. Add melted butter, egg and yolk, and gradually work into flour, using fingertips to form a soft and sticky ball of dough. Sift another ½ cup flour onto counter top. Gradually work flour and ½ cup water

LOIS WYSE

into dough, kneading until soft and elastic. Continue to add water until it is all incorporated. Knead dough (with heel of hand) about 5 minutes. Divide dough into 4 pieces. Wrap each piece in plastic wrap.

PREPARE PIEROGI:

Roll one piece of dough out on a floured surface to ⅛" thick circle. Cut circles in dough using a 3-inch cookie cutter or glass. Fill each circle with a heaping teaspoon of filling and fold dough over to form half-moons. Pinch closed tightly. Continue in this manner until all dough and filling have been used.

Drop pierogi, 10 at a time, into boiling salted water. They will float to the top when done, about 5 minutes. Remove with slotted spoon, drain in a colander. Or, over medium heat, lightly brown the boiled dumplings for 2–3 minutes on each side until golden and crisp.

SAVORY FILLING:

Any leftover minced meats (pork, beef, chicken, turkey, ham) or mushrooms can form the entire filling. Use your imagination.

FRUIT FILLING:

Pinch off small balls of dough. Stuff each with a slice of fresh purple plum, a whole strawberry dipped in sugar, or grated apple mixed with sugar, cinnamon, and raisins.

Hot Bacon-Horseradish Dip

Grandmothers schooled in the art of the leftover know that dips make good use of yesterday's dinner (or remnants of weekend breakfasts).

MAKES 1 CUP

4 strips bacon
1 8-ounce package cream cheese, softened
½ cup mayonnaise
2 scallions, finely chopped

1–2 teaspoons white horseradish
pinch white pepper
pinch cayenne pepper
¼ cup sliced or slivered almonds

Preheat oven to 375 degrees.

Sauté bacon until crisp. Drain and crumble. Mix cream cheese, mayonnaise, scallions, horseradish, and peppers in a small bowl. Stir in bacon and mix well. Transfer to an oven-proof, shallow 10-inch gratin dish. Sprinkle almonds evenly over top. Bake 15 minutes until brown and bubbly. Serve with crackers or chips.

Lois Wyse

S O U P S

REMEMBER WHAT IT WAS LIKE WHEN YOU STAYED HOME FROM SCHOOL PROPPED UP IN BED (TWO PILLOWS BEHIND YOUR STUFFY LITTLE HEAD), and were allowed to do all those special things like listen to the radio (my generation), watch TV (my children's generation), or use the computer (my grandchildren's generation)? In our day we'd hear and see all those dishy soap operas, and our mothers would bring us all kinds of special get-well foods. Comfort foods, we call them today.

Comfort foods are those certain foods that no one makes like a mother or grandmother.

High on the list is soup.

For some, it was Mama's chicken soup where noodles and the promise of quick recovery floated. For those whose families once lived in Scandinavian or Mediterranean countries, childhood memories come to a boil in fish soups. Fresh-caught fish was the base of the soup, and it changed daily, particularly if there were a fisherman in the household.

Soup was not a sometime course for many of our grandparents; it was as much a part of dinner as the meat or fish or poultry. Maybe that was because soup stretched for any family members who dropped by ("Add a cup of water, dear, your uncle's coming to supper").

Some of the soup recipes, as well as some other recipes, call for peeled tomatoes. If your grandmother didn't teach you the way to peel a tomato, here's how: Immerse the tomato in boiling water for 30 seconds, then plunge it into cold water and peel.

In collecting this group of recipes we've tried to soup up old favorites and find some charming new ones that will warm your heart and memory.

SOUPS

Mushroom-and-Barley Soup

Miso Soup

Chilled Cream of Tomato Soup

Corn Chowder

Salmon Soup (Seljanka)

Beet Borscht

Chicken Soup with Matzo Balls

Chinese Egg-Drop Soup

Tortilla Soup (Sopa de Lima)

Chicken and Lentil Soup (Mulligatawny)

Potato and Kale Soup with Sausage (Caldo Verde)

Beef Goulash Soup

Split-Pea Soup with Garlic Croutons

Oxtail Soup

Mushroom-and-Barley Soup

What is more comforting than coming home on a cold winter's night and finding steaming bowls of mushroom-barley soup waiting? Any kind of mushroom soup is a comfort food for all ages. This particular recipe began with Bubbie Becky in Russia, and came to us in English translation from her granddaughter Sherri. I like it because this version, which uses dried mushrooms and canned chicken stock, gives more flavor and is easier for contemporary cooks.

MAKES 6 TO 8 SERVINGS

1 ounce dried mushrooms
2 tablespoons olive oil
1 medium onion, chopped
2 cloves garlic, finely chopped
1 stalk of celery, chopped
1 carrot, peeled and chopped
1 medium potato, peeled and diced
1½ pounds white mushrooms, thinly
  sliced

⅓ cup pearl barley
1 bay leaf
1 teaspoon dried thyme
8 cups chicken stock
1 tablespoon each chopped fresh parsley
  and dill, for garnish

Soak mushrooms in 1 cup boiling water for 15 minutes. Drain, and reserve soaking liquid. Chop mushrooms. Strain liquid through cheesecloth to remove any grit or sand and set aside.

In a large stockpot, heat oil, and sauté onions, garlic, celery, carrot, potatoes, and white mushrooms over medium heat until softened, 5 to 6 minutes. Add dried mushrooms, barley, bay leaf, thyme, stock, and reserved mushroom liquid. Bring to a boil, cover, reduce heat to low, and simmer 45 minutes to 1 hour, or until barley is tender. Remove bay leaf before serving. Season with salt and pepper.

Garnish with fresh chopped parsley and dill.

Miso Soup

One thing about miso soup is that you don't have to be Japanese to love it. On a cold night it's a tummy warmer. On a hot day it's that one soup that restores the equilibrium and, who knows? It may even be good for the soul.

MAKES 6 TO 8 SERVINGS

4 large, dried, black mushrooms
1 carrot, sliced
2 cups chopped kale, napa cabbage,
    mustard greens, or other strongly
    flavored greens

¼ cup barley miso or rice (red) miso
¼ cup diced firm tofu
¼ cup chopped scallions, for garnish

Soak mushrooms in 6 cups water overnight. Strain liquid through cheesecloth into pot. Slice mushrooms and set aside.

Bring liquid to boil, add carrots, reduce heat to low, and simmer 10 minutes. Add greens, simmer 5 to 10 minutes. Add miso, diluting it first with a little of the broth. Remove from heat and let stand, 1 to 2 minutes.

Add sliced mushrooms. Put a teaspoon of tofu in bottom of each serving bowl, and top with soup and vegetables. Garnish with chopped scallions.

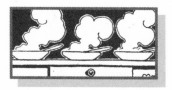

Lois Wyse

Chilled Cream of Tomato Soup

Jessie can't remember a time when she didn't love tomatoes because, to her, tomatoes meant her Italian grandmother's chilled cream of tomato soup. "We Italians make more than pasta," she reminds us, "because we know our tomatoes."

This soup is best made in the summer when tomatoes are at their peak of flavor.

MAKES 6 SERVINGS

2 pounds very ripe beefsteak or plum
    tomatoes, rubbed with olive oil and
    halved
3 tablespoons unsalted butter
1 medium onion, chopped
1 small carrot, chopped
1 small bulb of fennel, chopped
    (optional)

2 cups chicken stock
6 sprigs each fresh parsley and tarragon,
    tied together with string
Salt and freshly ground black pepper
    to taste
1 cup buttermilk
fresh chopped dill, for garnish

Preheat oven to 425 degrees.

Place tomatoes on greased baking pan and bake 30 minutes, turning tomatoes every 10 minutes until skins blister and blacken. Allow to cool, peel and discard skins, reserving pulp and juice.

Melt butter in a medium saucepan and sauté onion, carrot, and fennel, if using, on low heat, until very soft, 5 to 6 minutes. Add stock and herb bundle; simmer 30 minutes.

Remove herb bundle, add tomato pulp and juices. Allow soup to cool and puree in food processor. Add salt, pepper, and buttermilk.

Serve *well chilled*, sprinkled with fresh dill.

VARIATION

To serve hot: Replace the buttermilk with an equal amount of half-and-half.

Corn Chowder

"My Iowa grandmother made this with corn we grew, and she pretty much found the other vegetables on the farm," Ginny explains, "but I will admit I have added a granddaughter touch: jalapeño pepper." Not to worry, Ginny. Even if Grandmother wouldn't forgive you, we will. It does add zing to the chowder.

MAKES 8 SERVINGS

2 tablespoons butter or corn oil

1 onion, chopped

1 leek, white only, chopped

1 stalk celery, chopped

2 medium Idaho potatoes, peeled and
  chopped

8 cups vegetable stock or cold water

2 ears corn

1 small red bell pepper, seeded and finely
  diced

1 small jalapeño pepper, seeded and
  finely diced (optional)

1 zucchini, finely diced

1 yellow squash, finely diced

2 large carrots, peeled and finely diced

salt and freshly ground pepper to taste

1 teaspoon fresh chopped parsley, plus
  additional for garnish

1 teaspoon fresh chopped cilantro

dash cayenne pepper

1 cup cream, optional

In deep soup pot, over medium heat, heat butter and sauté onion, leek, celery, and potatoes until soft and golden but not browned. Add stock, reduce heat to low, cover, and simmer 15 minutes.

Puree soup in food processor or blender, until smooth. Return to pot. Cut and scrape corn kernels and their juices from cobs into small bowl. Add corn, peppers, zucchini, squash, and carrots to soup pot. Cover and cook an additional 10 minutes over medium heat.

Season with salt and pepper, parsley, cilantro, and cayenne. If desired, add cream and serve hot, garnished with parsley.

SERVING SUGGESTION

Add 1 cup fresh cooked crab or shrimp just before serving, to make a one-dish meal.

Salmon Soup

(Seljanka)

Sometimes, in our effort to pay homage to Russia's most famous soup, borscht, we forget that Russian grandmothers also made an extraordinary salmon soup. In the cold waters of their country salmon was plentiful, so this kind of good soup was a common alternative to its more famous beet cousin. Rhoda, now a grandmother herself, found this recipe in her grandmother's kitchen.

MAKES 8 TO 10 SERVINGS

2 tablespoons butter

2 scallions, julienned

1 knob celery root, peeled and julienned

1 medium carrot, julienned

2 cloves of garlic, crushed

2 quarts fish stock (recipe follows)

2 tablespoons tomato paste

1 bouquet garni (sprig of thyme, blade of
	mace, bay leaf, and 6 peppercorns
	tied inside a small piece of
	cheesecloth)

1 pound fresh salmon filet, skinned and
	boned, cut into small pieces

¼ cup sliced green olives

1 tablespoon capers

sour cream, for garnish

In deep soup pot, heat butter and sauté scallion, knob celery, carrots, and garlic until soft but not browned. Add stock, tomato paste, and *bouquet garni*. Simmer over low heat until vegetables are tender, about 20 minutes. Add salmon, olives, and capers. Simmer until fish has cooked through, about 1 to 2 minutes. Remove bouquet garni and adjust seasoning with salt and pepper. Serve with a dollop of sour cream in each bowl.

FISH STOCK:

2 pounds salmon bones and heads, 1 leek, white only, 1 onion, coarsely chopped, 2 sprigs parsley. Combine all the ingredients in a covered soup pot and simmered in 2 quarts water and 1 cup dry white wine, 45 minutes to an hour. Strain through cheesecloth.

Beet Borscht

And here for all who remember Russian grandmothers is our favorite recipe for borscht from Grandmother Malcha. It's surprisingly simple, too.

MAKES 6 SERVINGS

6 fresh beets, medium size, well scrubbed (about 3 pounds)
⅓ cup sugar
½ teaspoon salt

2 tablespoons lemon juice
⅓ cup sour cream
sour cream, boiled potatoes, fresh dill, for garnish

Put beets in a pot with 5 cups of water and cook until tender, 30 to 40 minutes. Drain beets, reserve water, and, while they are still warm, peel and slice over small bowl, saving any juice. Put two beets and juice into a blender or food processor and puree. Dice remaining beets.

Heat sugar, salt, lemon juice, and one cup of water in a saucepan until sugar has dissolved. Remove from heat, and stir in beet puree. Adjust seasoning, add reserved cooking liquid and diced beets. Whisk in sour cream.

Borscht should be served cold with a hot boiled potato in the center and an additional dollop of sour cream. Sprinkle with a few snips of fresh dill to garnish.

Lois Wyse

Chicken Soup with Matzo Balls

Sherri's favorite story about this fabled soup involves the granddaughter who asked her granny how to make chicken soup with matzo balls. Her grandmother gave her the recipe and cautioned, "First, you clean the chicken."

The granddaughter, eager to do her best, promptly took out her can of kitchen cleanser and *scrubbed* the chicken until it shone. Then she called her grandmother. "Grandma," she said proudly, "I not only cleaned the chicken, I scoured it."

MAKES 8 TO 10 SERVINGS

1 3–4 pound chicken, quartered
2 large stalks celery, cut into chunks
1 large onion, quartered
2 large leeks, whites only, well washed and cut into chunks
4 large carrots, cut into chunks
1 large parsnip, cut into chunks

1 handful fresh dill, thick stems trimmed away
1 handful fresh parsley, thick stems trimmed away
2 teaspoons salt, or to taste
½ teaspoon whole black peppercorns

Rinse chicken and place in large soup pot with the celery, onion, leeks, carrots, parsnips, dill, parsley, salt, and pepper. Add 4 quarts cold water. Bring to a boil and reduce heat to simmer. Cover pot partially, leaving the lid ajar so steam can escape. Be sure stock never boils or it will become cloudy. Simmer 1 to 1½ hours.

Allow stock to cool. Remove chicken. Reserve meat for another use, or serve with soup. Strain stock through fine cheesecloth, reserve carrots, if desired, and discard the solids. Return carrots to stock and refrigerate overnight. The following day remove and discard fat which will have risen to surface.

continued on next page

FLUFFY MATZO BALLS

MAKES 8 TO 10 MATZO BALLS

2 eggs
4 tablespoons melted chicken fat or
    salad oil

2 tablespoons club soda or seltzer
1 teaspoon salt
1 cup matzo meal

Put eggs, fat or oil, soda, and salt together in a bowl and beat well. Stir in matzo meal, adding just enough to make a stiff mixture. Chill at least one hour.

Bring a large pot of salted water to a boil. Wet hands and form mixture into medium-size balls. Drop balls into boiling water and immediately reduce heat to simmer. Cover and cook 30 minutes. Remove from water with slotted spoon, and add matzo balls to chicken soup.

TO SERVE:

Reheat the soup.

Put one matzo ball in the bottom of each soup bowl. Ladle the soup over, and serve immediately.

Lois Wyse

Chinese Egg-Drop Soup

Some years ago, my husband and I took a Chinese cooking class in a friend's home. One of the first things we learned was to go to market in Chinatown. There is a difference in poultry and vegetables (as well as seasonings) to be found there. So if you're in or near a large city, start your recipe with a trip to Chinatown—or a reasonable facsimile—for your groceries.

MAKES 6 TO 8 SERVINGS

1 4–5 pound chicken, rinsed

1 medium onion, quartered

3 carrots, sliced

1 teaspoon salt

1 tablespoon cornstarch, dissolved in 2 tablespoons cold water

2 scallions, cut into ⅛-inch pieces

1 thick slice boiled ham (about ¼ pound), cut into julienne

2 eggs, beaten

pinch white pepper

Put chicken in large soup pot with two quarts of water. Add onion and carrots. Cover, and bring to boil. Reduce heat to low, simmer one hour. Add salt and cook until chicken is tender, about one hour more.

Remove the chicken and reserve for another use. Cool soup, strain and skim off fat. Discard solids.

TO SERVE:

Heat broth. Whisk in cornstarch mixture. Stir in scallions and ham. Slowly stir in beaten egg. Turn off heat *immediately*, allowing egg to float gently to the surface. Finish with a pinch of white pepper. Serve immediately.

Tortilla Soup

(Sopa de Lima)

Mexican grandmothers know that the tortilla is the staff of life, so it is only appropriate that we include a tortilla soup. Consuela assures us that this is a real grandmother soup, because it's a good-tasting way to make use of day-old tortillas. Just call this the chicken soup of Mexico.

MAKES 8 SERVINGS

2 tablespoons corn oil

4 corn tortillas, shredded

2 cloves garlic, minced

1 small onion, chopped

1 small jalapeño pepper, seeded and
  diced

4 large ripe tomatoes, peeled, seeded, and
  chopped

2 tablespoons tomato paste

2 teaspoons ground cumin

1 teaspoon ground coriander

1 teaspoon salt

¼ teaspoon ground cayenne pepper

freshly ground black pepper

8 cups chicken stock (preferably
  homemade)

GARNISH:

1 tablespoon corn oil

2 corn tortillas, cut into thin strips

1 ripe avocado, peeled and diced

2 ears corn, kernels cut off cob and
  steamed until tender

1 large ripe tomato, peeled, seeded, and
  diced

½ cup grated Monterey Jack cheese

2 tablespoons chopped fresh cilantro

2 tablespoons chopped fresh parsley

sour cream, optional

Lois Wyse

In deep soup pot, over high heat, heat corn oil and sauté tortillas briefly until crisp. Add garlic, onion, and jalapeño pepper. Cook I to 2 minutes more. Reduce heat to low, add tomatoes, paste, and cumin, coriander, salt, and peppers, and cook another 10 minutes. Add the stock and cook, uncovered, 20 minutes.

Cool slightly. Puree soup in food processor or blender until smooth.

Before serving, reheat soup and prepare garnishes. Heat corn oil and sauté tortilla strips until crisp. In a small bowl, mix avocado, corn, and tomato. Put a spoonful of chopped vegetables in each bowl of soup. Top with grated cheese and chopped herbs. Sprinkle with tortilla strips and finish with a dollop of sour cream, if desired.

Chicken and Lentil Soup

(Mulligatawny)

Mulligatawny was brought back to England by those who were posted in India when the British Empire held sway over the world. Until that time, English palates were not acquainted with the exotic spices of the world. Our recipe comes from Penelope whose grandparents lived in India for twenty years. Although the recipe calls for homemade chicken stock, it is possible to use canned chicken broth—but you will lose the true grand-mother touch, because in the Indian version a whole chicken is used.

MAKES 8 SERVINGS

1 cup red lentils
6 cups chicken stock, preferably
    homemade
2–3 cloves garlic, minced
1 teaspoon minced fresh ginger
1 large Idaho potato, peeled and diced
½ teaspoon salt

1 teaspoon ground cumin
1 teaspoon ground coriander
¼ teaspoon cayenne pepper
½ teaspoon ground turmeric
1 whole boned and skinless chicken
    breast, cut into cubes or shreds
lemon slices, for garnish

In large soup pot, bring lentils and stock to a boil. Reduce heat, simmer 30 minutes.

In a small bowl, mix garlic and ginger together with a few tablespoons of water (or extra stock) to form a thick paste. Stir into soup pot. Add potatoes, and simmer 20 minutes.

Puree soup in blender or food processor, and return to soup pot. Bring to a simmer and stir in the salt, cumin, coriander, cayenne, and turmeric. Add additional stock or water if soup is too thick. Add chicken and, over medium heat, continue to cook 10 to 15 minutes more, or until chicken pieces are cooked through.

Serve hot with a slice of lemon or squeeze in 1 tablespoon of fresh lemon juice just before serving.

Lois Wyse

Potato and Kale Soup with Sausage
(Caldo Verde)

*C*aldo verde is the peasant soup of Portugal and, like almost all peasant soups, it is an all-day soup. In the morning, the pot is put on the stove and left to simmer. By dinnertime, the soup is ready. Often, the pot stays on the stove for days. Each day Grandmother adds the leftovers of that meal—bits of vegetables, bones, scraps, and by week's end it may be the same pot, but it's a whole new soup.

MAKES 8 SERVINGS

½ cup dried white lima beans
4 ounces smoked pork garlic sausage,
    preferably chorizo or kielbasa
6 tablespoons olive oil
2 medium Spanish onions, cut into thin
    wedges

2 potatoes
½ pound fresh kale, collard greens, or
    green cabbage
Salt and freshly ground black pepper

Soak beans overnight in a bowl of cold water to cover by two inches over. Drain beans.

Prick sausages and place in a small skillet. Cover with water and bring to a boil. Reduce heat, simmer 15 minutes. Drain sausages on paper towels and slice into ½-inch rounds.

In large soup pot, over medium heat, heat oil, and add onions. Sauté, stirring occasionally, until golden, about 3 minutes. Add 3 cups of water, potatoes, and beans. Bring to a boil, reduce heat, and simmer one hour. Season with salt and pepper.

Trim greens, remove tough stems, and shred. Add greens to the soup with three more cups of water, and simmer 1½ hours more. Add sausage during the last half hour of cooking time. Adjust seasoning before serving.

Beef Goulash Soup

As a child with a Hungarian grandmother, I knew how goulash was supposed to taste, but as an adult I never tasted goulash like my grandmother's until I went to Budapest, and a friend gave me this recipe.

MAKES 8 TO 10 SERVINGS

4 tablespoons vegetable oil

2 pounds of boneless beef chuck, trimmed, cut into 1-inch dice

4 medium onions, chopped

4 cloves of garlic, minced

⅓ cup all-purpose flour

3 tablespoons sweet Hungarian paprika

¼ cup red-wine vinegar

1 14-ounce can crushed tomatoes

4 cups beef stock, preferably homemade

¼ teaspoon marjoram

½ teaspoon each salt and pepper

2 large potatoes, peeled and cut into ½" dice

chopped parsley, for garnish.

In large soup pot, heat 2 tablespoons oil, and brown beef over high heat. Remove meat with slotted spoon and set aside.

Reduce heat to medium. Heat remaining oil. Add onions and garlic and sauté until golden. Stir in flour and paprika, cook 2 minutes. Pour in vinegar and tomatoes and stir vigorously for about 1 minute while mixture thickens.

Add stock, 4 cups water, marjoram, salt, pepper, and meat. Bring to a boil, cover, and simmer 45 minutes. Stir in potatoes and simmer 30 minutes.

Adjust seasoning and add additional water or stock if the soup has become too thick. Serve soup hot with a sprinkle of chopped fresh parsley.

Lois Wyse

Split-Pea Soup with Garlic Croutons

Not only does a ham provide a good dinner and leftovers for sandwiches, there's that ham bone for pea soup. A good pea soup stays in the refrigerator (keep it in a glass jar, not plastic) for many days and gets better and better. Aliza says she knows it must be winter when she sees the jar of pea soup in her fridge just waiting for a hungry grandchild to arrive. And on cold days, what better way to warm a guest (or yourself)?

MAKES 8 SERVINGS

8 cups chicken stock

1 cup dried green split peas

3 onions, chopped

3 carrots, diced

2 stalks celery, chopped

1 pound ham hocks (or ham bone)

2 large potatoes, peeled and diced

2 bay leaves

Salt and freshly ground pepper

In large soup pot, bring stock to a boil. Add peas, onions, carrots, celery, ham, potatoes, and bay leaves. Reduce heat and simmer one hour. Remove the ham hocks and bay leaves. Allow soup to cool slightly.

Puree half the soup in a blender or food processor. Return puree to soup pot.

Trim meat from bones of ham hocks, add to soup. Discard bones. Heat soup and season with salt and pepper. Float a crouton (or two) on top of each serving, if desired.

GARLIC CROUTONS

1 stick unsalted butter

4 cloves garlic, peeled and cut in half

8 1-inch slices French bread

Preheat oven to 350 degrees.

Heat butter and garlic together in a small pan. Allow to sit a few minutes. Place bread slices on a cookie sheet. Brush with butter and bake 15 minutes, or until crisp and golden.

Oxtail Soup

A German grandmother who makes magic in her kitchen (even with oxtails) came up with this recipe. Her granddaughter thinks it's the best soup in the world. She just may be right.

2 pounds oxtails

2 tablespoons all-purpose flour

2 tablespoons vegetable oil

1 large onion, diced

1 pound white mushrooms, trimmed and
  sliced

4 garlic cloves, minced

4 large carrots, peeled and cut into
  chunks

2 stalks celery, thickly sliced

1 large parsnip, peeled, cut into chunks

1 large Idaho potato, cut into chunks

1 16-ounce can crushed tomatoes

½ teaspoon dried oregano

½ teaspoon dried basil

¼ teaspoon dried thyme

2 bay leaves

1 cup red wine

½ teaspoon salt

½ teaspoon freshly ground black pepper

chopped parsley for garnish

Lightly flour oxtails, shaking off any excess. Over medium heat, heat oil in soup pot, and lightly brown meat. Add onions, mushrooms, and garlic and sauté a few minutes, until soft. Add carrot, celery, parsnip, potato, tomatoes, oregano, basil, thyme, and bay leaves.

Pour in wine and add enough cold water to cover. Bring to a boil and reduce to simmer. Cover pot and cook 2 hours. Add salt, pepper, and chopped parsley. Remove bay leaves before serving.

Lois Wyse

F I S H

EVER SINCE THE WORDS *CHOLESTEROL* AND *FATS* CAME INTO OUR VOCABULARY, FISH HAS BEEN A CONTEMPORARY DISH. OUR GRANDMOTHERS' FISH recipes originated in Scandinavia, in the Mediterranean—and in the United States, too, where the catfish, whitefish, and trout taste better than practically anywhere else on earth.

Fish was not always a main dish in Grandmother's house; often it was a separate course that preceded the main event—the roast or poultry specialty of the house.

So, we offer fish as either a first or main course. Friday night fish fries are a highlight of life in the Midwest; gumbos, a Southern specialty; and, as any Gulf Coast resident knows, there isn't a family that doesn't have a recipe for memorable crab cakes.

Yet, no matter where she lived, every grandmother had the same secret for all fish cookery. It was simply to make sure that the fish was fresh. For, as every grandmother has taught us, "Fish and guests spoil after three days."

FISH

Crab Cakes with Rémoulade Sauce

Salmon Patties with Dill Sauce

Baked Shrimp with Feta Cheese (Shrimp Santorini)

Shrimp Gumbo

Sweet 'n' Sour Cod

Bacalhau

Pan-Fried Trout

Friday Night Fish Fry

Baked Whitefish Fillets

Fisherman's Pie

Crab Cakes
with Rémoulade Sauce

Greg grew up in New Orleans, and that's where his grandmother made her crab cakes. He admits that it's not the first thing that comes to mind when one thinks of Creole cooking, but he's sure that there must have been a sea captain in the family tree. All of which proves that grandmother cooking isn't always what it seems to be. No matter the grandmother's origins, however, one thing she always uses in crab cakes is Old Bay Seasoning. From Baltimore to New Orleans, there's no substitute for that.

MAKES 6 TO 8 SERVINGS

2 pounds fresh lump crabmeat
⅔ cup coarsely crushed Saltine crackers
2 tablespoons pimento, chopped
2 tablespoons fresh parsley, chopped
2 teaspoons Old Bay Seasoning, or
    seafood seasoning of your choice
2 eggs, lightly beaten
1–2 tablespoons Dijon mustard
2 teaspoons Worcestershire sauce

2–3 dashes Tabasco
1 cup fine breadcrumbs (Wondra flour
    may be substituted)
2–3 tablespoons butter
½ cup whipped cream,
    optional
1 cup rémoulade sauce (recipe
    follows)

Carefully pick over crabmeat to remove cartilage. Put into bowl with crushed crackers, pimento, parsley, and seafood seasoning. Mix in eggs, mustard, Worcestershire, and Tabasco. Wet hands and form mixture into 12–14 small patties. Chill 30 minutes.

Lightly coat patties in breadcrumbs. Over high heat, heat butter in skillet and sauté patties until crisp and golden brown, 2 to 3 minutes on each side. Add more butter to pan, as needed.

Fold whipped cream (optional) into rémoulade sauce. Serve cakes with sauce and lemon wedges.

continued on next page

RÉMOULADE SAUCE

MAKES 2 CUPS

2 cups mayonnaise, preferably homemade

1 tablespoon chopped sweet pickle

1 tablespoon capers (optional)

1 tablespoon chopped shallots

1 teaspoon dried tarragon

2 hard-boiled eggs, finely chopped

1 teaspoon Dijon mustard

1 tablespoon finely chopped parsley

1 teaspoon mashed anchovy or anchovy
*   paste*

freshly ground black pepper to taste

Mix all ingredients together in a bowl. Chill before serving.

MAYONNAISE

MAKES 1 CUP

2 egg yolks

1 teaspoon Dijon mustard

3 teaspoons fresh squeezed lemon juice

dash each salt, white pepper, and cayenne
*   pepper*

1 cup vegetable oil

In small bowl, whisk together yolks, mustard, lemon juice, salt, and peppers. Begin adding oil, drop by drop, whisking until mixture begins to thicken. Add remaining oil in slow, steady stream until all is incorporated. Adjust seasoning with salt, pepper, or lemon juice.

Lois Wyse

Salmon Patties with Dill Sauce

During the Depression, housewives had to think of inexpensive ways to feed their families. One friend recalls that his grandmother made onions so often and with so many different recipes that her family nicknamed her "Frying Pan Annie." Stews and soups were popular, and so were dishes making use of food extenders such as breadcrumbs or crackers. In the summertime, when the corn was high and plentiful, salmon patties were often served. Ruthanne says she can't think of the Depression without tasting salmon patties. Here's her recipe.

MAKES 4 SERVINGS

1 1-pound can Alaskan sockeye salmon, drained well, or 1 pound fresh, poached salmon

¼ cup milk

2 slices white bread, crust removed and cubed

2 eggs, lightly beaten

1 tablespoon minced onion

1 tablespoon chopped fresh parsley

¼ teaspoon salt

freshly ground black pepper to taste

3–4 tablespoons butter

dill sauce (recipe follows)

lemon wedges and parsley, for garnish

Remove any bone, cartilage, or skin from fish. Transfer to bowl and mash with a fork. In a separate bowl, pour milk over bread and soak until soft. Squeeze excess moisture from bread and add to salmon. Mix in remaining milk, eggs, onion, parsley, salt, and pepper. If mixture is too loose, add another egg or a bit more bread. Form mixture into patties, using about 2 tablespoons per patty. Heat skillet, add butter and drop in patty. Fry a few minutes per side until crisp and golden brown. Serve with dill sauce. Garnish with lemon wedges and parsley.

DILL SAUCE

MAKES 2 CUPS

1 cup mayonnaise, preferably homemade (see page 56)

1 cup sour cream

1 teaspoon fresh lemon juice

2 teaspoons fresh dill, snipped

1 teaspoon fresh parsley, chopped

½ teaspoon salt

freshly ground black pepper to taste

Blend all ingredients well. Chill before serving.

Baked Shrimp with Feta Cheese

(Shrimp Santorini)

Anastasia's memories of Greece include going to the tavernas on the island of Santorini as the fishing boats arrived with the catch of the day. Can our Shrimp Santorini, even when made far from the seacoast, come out quite the same? Probably not—but add enough tomatoes and feta when you cook and you'll taste the tradition.

MAKES 6 TO 8 SERVINGS

2 tablespoons olive oil
1 onion, chopped
2 cloves garlic, minced
5 pounds ripe tomatoes, peeled, seeded, and chopped
1 tablespoon chopped fresh oregano or 1 teaspoon dried
1 tablespoon chopped fresh basil
2 tablespoons chopped fresh parsley

½ cup dry white wine
½ teaspoon salt
freshly ground black pepper to taste
2 tablespoons capers
3 pounds fresh shrimp, peeled and deveined (about 48)
1 pound feta cheese, diced
Sprinkle of grated Parmesan cheese

Preheat oven to 400 degrees. Heat oil in skillet, add onions and garlic, sauté 2–3 minutes. Add tomatoes, oregano, basil, parsley, wine, salt, and pepper. Cook, uncovered, over medium heat, to reduce liquid, about 10 minutes. Continue to cook 10 minutes more, or until mixture becomes a thickened tomato sauce. Remove from heat, and stir in capers.

Spoon 2 tablespoons of sauce over bottom of a 2-quart ovenproof glass baking dish. Scatter on shrimp and cover with remaining sauce. Sprinkle with feta and Parmesan. Bake 20 minutes, or until cheese has browned. Garnish top with chopped parsley before serving. Serve with hot, crusty bread for dunking.

Lois Wyse

Shrimp Gumbo

Elizabeth grew up in New Orleans, and remembers the way her grandmother, small and frail, got up at 5 A.M. to cook Creole dishes for the family. By the time the family awakened, the whole house was full of the smells of Grandmother's cooking. Although she was tiny, the mighty granny lifted and turned her big cast-iron pots with ease. Because her grandmother lived with the family for some years, Elizabeth had a chance to watch her grandmother cook and learned her recipes.

MAKES 8 SERVINGS

¾ cup plus 3 tablespooons
    butter
¾ cup all-purpose flour
1 clove garlic, minced
2 stalks celery, chopped
1 onion, chopped
2 bell peppers, 1 red and 1 green, seeded
    and diced
½ teaspoon dried red-pepper flakes
2 teaspoons chili powder
1 pound fresh tomatoes, chopped (or 1
    14-ounce can, chopped)
4 cups each chicken stock and cold water
½ pound fresh okra, sliced (frozen may be
    substituted)

2 teaspoons Worcestershire sauce
1 teaspoon Tabasco sauce
1 teaspoon dried thyme
1 teaspoon dried marjoram
1 teaspoon dried oregano
½ teaspoon dried sage
2 teaspoons salt
1 teaspoon freshly ground black pepper
2 teaspoons sugar
juice of 1 lemon
3 pounds fresh shrimp, peeled and
    deveined
1 cup chopped scallions

In heavy saucepan, melt ¾ cup butter until foamy. Whisk in flour and cook over very low heat, until mixture becomes a golden amber, about 10 minutes. Remove from heat and set aside. This mixture is called a roux.

In a soup pot, melt 3 tablespoons butter. Add garlic, celery, onion, peppers, pepper flakes, and chili powder. Sauté about 5 minutes. Add the roux, slowly. Add the tomatoes, stock, water, okra, Worcestershire sauce, Tabasco, thyme, marjoram, oregano, sage, salt, pepper, sugar, and lemon juice. Cover pot, simmer 45 minutes. Add shrimp and scallions for final 15 minutes, or until shrimp are cooked.

Sweet 'n' Sour Cod

This is a recipe Italian grandmothers loved to make for their families. The only difference is they didn't use canned tomatoes, but our Italian friend Mary, who gave us this recipe, promises that her Italian-born mother-in-law doesn't object when she does.

MAKES 8 SERVINGS

4 tablespoons olive oil
2 large onions, thinly sliced
2 1-pound, 12-ounce cans Italian plum
    tomatoes, drained and chopped,
    liquid reserved
Zest and juice of 1 large navel orange
¼ cup dry sherry
¼ cup apple-cider vinegar

¼ cup dark-brown sugar
1 bay leaf
1 cinnamon stick
salt and freshly ground black pepper to
    taste
2 pounds cod fillets, cut into 8 pieces
¼ cup all-purpose flour

In a large saucepan, heat 2 tablespoons oil, add onions, and cook over low heat until soft and golden, about 10 minutes. Add the tomatoes, orange juice, zest, sherry, vinegar, sugar, bay leaf, cinnamon, salt, and pepper. Add 1 cup of the reserved tomato liquid and bring mixture to a boil. Reduce heat, simmer sauce 25 to 30 minutes. Add salt and pepper to taste. If sauce is not sweet enough, add more brown sugar. If too sweet, add more cider vinegar.

In a large skillet, heat remaining oil. Season flour with salt and pepper. Dip cod fillets in flour, shaking off excess. Lightly brown fish a few minutes on each side. Pour sauce over fish and cook until cod is done, about 10 minutes. Discard bay leaf and cinnamon stick before serving.

Lois Wyse

Bacalhau

*B*acalhau, a cherished dish in both Spanish and Italian families, is frequently served on Christmas Eve before church. It comes to us via Liza's Spanish husband's family.

MAKES 8 SERVINGS

3 pounds salt cod

6 large baking potatoes, peeled, and
    sliced

1 cup olive oil

3 large onions, finely chopped

3 cloves garlic, minced

1 6-ounce can tomato paste, diluted in 1
    cup water

½ teaspoon salt

6 hard-cooked eggs, peeled and sliced

1 cup black Spanish olives, for garnish

Soak cod in cold water to cover for 24 hours, changing water several times.

Preheat oven to 350 degrees.

Drain and rinse fish. Put in large pot and cover with boiling water. Cover pot and cook 20 to 30 minutes or until fish flakes easily. Drain and cool. Rinse pot, add potatoes, and cover with cold water. Bring to a boil, reduce heat, and cook 10 minutes until cooked but still firm. Drain and cool.

Heat oil in skillet, sauté onions and garlic over low heat until soft and golden, about 10 minutes. Add diluted tomato paste and salt. Mix well, remove from heat and set aside.

Flake fish carefully, removing any bones and skin. Layer a 9- x 13-inch ovenproof glass dish with potatoes, fish and sauce. Cover with egg slices and olives. If desired, drizzle with additional olive oil. Bake 30 to 45 minutes, until top is lightly browned.

Pan-Fried Trout

Carrie grew up in northern Michigan, and remembers that when her grandfather came home with the catch of the day, her grandmother would take out her boning knife, heat the frying pan, and then listen as Grandfather told how he'd landed this big one—but, oh, if only the family had seen the one that got away.

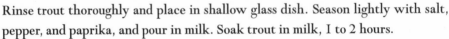

8 small, whole trout, cleaned, boned, and heads removed	2 cups all-purpose flour
salt, pepper, and paprika to taste	4 tablespoons butter
2 cups milk	4 tablespoons slivered or sliced almonds
	2 tablespoons fresh lemon juice
	1 tablespoon chopped fresh parsley

Rinse trout thoroughly and place in shallow glass dish. Season lightly with salt, pepper, and paprika, and pour in milk. Soak trout in milk, 1 to 2 hours.

Drain, pat dry slightly, and dip in flour to cover evenly, shaking off any excess. Heat butter in skillet until foamy. Fry trout until crisp and golden brown on each side, turning carefully so as not to disturb coating, 2 to 3 minutes. Transfer to serving platter. Add almonds to pan drippings, adding more butter if needed. Over medium heat, sauté 2 to 3 minutes. Stir in lemon juice and spoon sauce over trout. Garnish with chopped parsley.

Lois Wyse

Friday Night Fish Fry

Sherri has spent many nights in Wisconsin, where the Friday night fish isn't just a dinner; it is a great neighborhood party—noisy, not too formal and with plenty of room for kids and grannies.

MAKES 8 TO 10 SERVINGS

3–4 pounds mixed white fish fillets, such as perch, whitefish, haddock, cod, sole, or flounder
salt and pepper
2 cups all-purpose flour

2 cups beer batter (recipe follows)
4 cups solid vegetable shortening for deep frying
2 cups tartar sauce (recipe follows)

Rinse fillets under cold water and pat dry with paper towel. Cut larger fillets into long pieces, about 1–2 inches wide. Leave whole smaller fillets, such as perch. Season with salt and pepper and set aside.

Put the flour and batter in separate bowls for dipping. Heat shortening in deep fryer to 375 degrees or use deep pot with frying thermometer attached. Dredge fish in flour, shaking off excess.

Dip fish in batter and drop carefully into hot fat. Allow fish to fry until golden brown on all sides, about 5 minutes. Remove with slotted spoon. Drain on paper towel. Serve immediately with tartar sauce.

BEER BATTER

2 cans beer
2 cups all-purpose flour
1 teaspoon salt

1 teaspoon paprika
freshly ground black pepper, to taste

Beat ingredients together in a deep bowl with an egg beater or wire whisk until smooth. (This can also be done in a blender.) Chill in refrigerator for about one hour before using.

continued on next page

TARTAR SAUCE

2 cups mayonnaise, preferably homemade
    (page 56)
½ *small onion, finely chopped*
2 *shallots, finely chopped*
3–4 *midget gherkins or sweet pickle,*
    chopped

1 *teaspoon capers*
1 *teaspoon fresh parsley, chopped*
2 *teaspoons fresh chives, snipped*
dash Tabasco sauce
½ *teaspoon salt*
freshly ground black pepper, to taste

Mix ingredients together. Chill before serving.

Lois Wyse

Baked Whitefish Fillets

Although I grew up on the shores of Lake Erie, it was not until I moved away that I really appreciated the taste of the fish, particularly when baked. Sherri and Liza found this recipe in the kitchen of a Chicago grandmother.

Makes 8 servings

2 tablespoons butter
1 large onion, chopped
2 stalks celery, chopped
2 carrots, sliced
1 teaspoon chopped fresh parsley
1 teaspoon chopped fresh dill

2 ripe tomatoes, seeded and diced
8 whitefish fillets, bones and skin
   removed
salt and freshly ground black pepper to
   taste
1 cup whole milk or half-and-half

Preheat oven to 350 degrees.

In medium skillet, heat butter and sauté onion, celery, and carrots over low heat until onions are golden, about 5 minutes. Do not brown vegetables.

Mix in parsley, dill, and tomatoes. Spread mixture over bottom of 9- x 13-inch oven-proof glass dish. Lightly season fish, fold each fillet in half and place over vegetables. Add milk (or half-and-half) to barely cover fish. Leave tops of fillets exposed.

Bake casserole 20 minutes, or until fish flakes easily with a fork. Tops should be lightly browned and bubbly.

Fisherman's Pie

Gabbie's Belgian grandmother taught her how to make Sunday night suppers with this delicious and easy one-dish fisherman's pie. Gabbie now passes it along for everyone who wants to stay at home on Sunday night to watch Masterpiece Theatre.

MAKES 8 TO 10 SERVINGS

3 pounds white fish fillets, such as
   flounder, haddock, halibut, or sole
Salt and freshly ground black pepper to
   taste
4 cups milk
10 tablespoons butter
1 large onion, diced
½ pound boiled or baked ham, diced
6 tablespoons all-purpose flour
4 hard-cooked eggs, coarsely chopped

3 tablespoons chopped fresh parsley
2 tablespoons chopped fresh dill
1 tablespoon capers, drained well
   (optional)
1 tablespoon fresh lemon juice
3 pounds red-skinned potatoes, peeled
   and cubed
½ cup sour cream
dash nutmeg

Preheat oven to 400 degrees. Butter a 9- x 13-inch ovenproof glass baking dish, add fish fillets in one layer, season with salt and pepper. Cover with 1½ cups of the milk, seal with foil and bake until the fish flakes easily with a fork, about 15 minutes.

Using a slotted spoon, transfer fish to a bowl. Strain cooking liquid into a saucepan, cook over high heat, and reduce to 1½ cups. Set aside.

Lois Wyse

In the saucepan, melt 6 tablespoons of butter until foamy. Sauté onions and ham to soften, 2 to 3 minutes. Whisk in flour, stirring well. Gradually pour in remaining 2½ cups milk and reserved cooking liquid, whisking well. Season with salt and pepper. Continue cooking until sauce comes to a boil and thickens, about 5 minutes.

Remove from heat and stir in eggs, parsley, dill, capers, and lemon juice. Flake fish with a fork and fold into sauce.

Cook potatoes in cold water to cover until very tender, about 20 minutes. Drain, and beat or mash potatoes. Add remaining 4 tablespoons butter, sour cream, nutmeg, and salt and pepper to taste and continue to beat until very smooth.

Spoon fish mixture into buttered shallow 3-quart baking dish. Spread evenly and cover with mashed potatoes. Bake until top is lightly browned and edges are bubbly, about 35 to 40 minutes.

Cool pie for a few minutes before cutting and serving.

POULTRY

ANY GRANDMOTHER WORTHY OF THE NAME KNOWS AT LEAST SIXTEEN WAYS TO MAKE CHICKEN. PER-HAPS THAT IS BECAUSE OUR GRANDMOTHERS' grandmothers all learned that the fastest way to get dinner was to go to the henhouse. No matter what her nationality, a granddaughter might re-call a grandmother standing at the kitchen sink carefully singeing the chicken to rid it of pinfeathers. Our grandmothers always had an eye on the purse strings, so they made use of every part of the chicken: the feet went into the stock, fat was rendered, the giblets made the gravy, the neck was roasted and given to the smallest child, and even the "parson's nose" found its way to someone's plate.

The recipes included here represent only a small portion of the poultry recipes we collected.

POULTRY

Chicken Pot Pie

Fried Chicken and Biscuits

Poulet Grandmere

Brunswick Stew

Chicken-and-Rice Casserole (Arroz con Pollo)

Basque Chicken

Chicken Cacciatore

Chicken and Cornbread Dressing
(Preacher's Sunday Night Supper)

Chicken Spaghetti

Chicken Egg Foo Yoong

Chicken Paprikash

Chicken Fricassee with Parsley Dumplings

Roast Duck with Red Cabbage and Spatzle

Sausage and Chestnut Dressing for Poultry

Chicken Pot Pie

There has been a renaissance of home cooking recently. Notice how many restaurants now feature mashed potatoes, meat loaf, and other good old farm food? One of the old-time favorites is this chicken pot pie from an Indiana grandmother.

1 2–3 pound frying chicken, quartered

1 onion, chopped

2 carrots, sliced

2 stalks celery, sliced

4 sprigs fresh parsley

1½ teaspoons salt

1 cup dry white wine

6 tablespoons butter

8 tablespoons all-purpose flour

1½ cups milk

¼ teaspoon white pepper

¼ teaspoon cayenne pepper

dash nutmeg

¼ cup heavy cream (optional)

1 large onion, peeled and diced

3 carrots, peeled and diced

2 Idaho potatoes, peeled and diced

1 pound fresh mushrooms, trimmed and sliced

1 10-ounce package frozen green peas, defrosted

2 tablespoons chopped fresh parsley

1 tablespoon snipped fresh dill

For PASTRY

2 cups all-purpose flour

½ teaspoon salt

8 tablespoons butter

4 tablespoons solid vegetable shortening

1–2 tablespoons ice water

Put chicken in soup pot. Add onion, carrots, celery, and parsley. Add 2 quarts cold water and 1 teaspoon salt, cover, and bring to a boil. Reduce heat and simmer 1 hour. Remove chicken, drain and cool. Strain stock, discarding solids. Put 2 cups of stock in saucepan. Add wine, cook over high heat until liquid is reduced to 2 cups. Set aside. When chicken is cool enough to handle, remove skin and bones and cut meat into large dice. Set aside.

Make the pastry. Put flour and salt into large mixing bowl. Blend in butter, little bits at a time, using a pastry cutter or two forks. Add shortening and mix with fingertips until crumbly. Add ice water, 1 tablespoon at a time, and knead dough until it forms a soft ball. Wrap dough in wax paper. Chill until ready to use.

Heat 4 tablespoons butter in a saucepan until hot and foamy. Whisk in flour, stirring well to form a paste, or roux. Whisk in reduced stock and milk and continue whisking to remove lumps. Cook until mixture comes to a boil and thickens. Add ½ teaspoon salt, pepper, nutmeg, and cream. Set aside.

Heat 2 tablespoons butter in skillet. Sauté onions, carrots, potatoes, and mushrooms until golden, but not brown. Stir in peas, parsley, and dill, and remove from heat.

Preheat oven to 375 degrees. Have ready a 9- x 13-inch ovenproof glass baking dish (or six individual 12-ounce glass baking dishes). Mix sautéed vegetables with sauce and stir in chicken pieces. Spoon mixture into baking dish.

On a lightly floured board, roll out large rectangle of pastry, 1 inch larger than baking dish, to thickness of ⅛ inch. Lay dough over filling and press edges firmly to rim of dish. Flute pastry edges attractively. Cut three or four ½-inch circles in top of crust to act as vents. This will prevent pastry from bursting during baking. If using individual dishes, one vent will be sufficient. Brush top lightly with milk. Bake until golden brown and bubbling, about 30 minutes.

Fried Chicken and Biscuits

If you put 100 grandmothers in a room, you will get 100 recipes for fried chicken. How do we know? Because we did it! The reason we selected this recipe is that buttermilk gives it a distinctive piquancy. So add it to your recipe box.

MAKES 8 SERVINGS

2 2½–3 pound frying chickens, cut into
    serving pieces
salt, black pepper, and paprika
2 cups buttermilk
2 cups all-purpose flour, more if needed

8 tablespoons butter
8 tablespoons solid vegetable shortening
¼ cup water
buttermilk biscuits (recipe follows)

Rinse chicken, pat dry with paper towel. Season lightly with salt, pepper, and paprika, and place in a shallow dish. Soak chicken in buttermilk and refrigerate several hours or overnight. Bring to room temperature before frying.

    Put flour in deep bowl. Lift chicken out of buttermilk and drop into flour. Turn chicken over several times to coat well. Do not shake off excess. Heat butter, shortening, and water in a two deep skillets until very hot. Carefully drop chicken in hot fat, starting with dark meat. Reduce heat if chicken is browning too quickly. Do not overcrowd skillets. Fry, turning often, until chicken is crispy and golden brown, about 20 minutes. Transfer to cookie sheet and keep warm in 250 degree oven.

BUTTERMILK BISCUITS

MAKES 8 BISCUITS

2 cups all-purpose flour
½ teaspoon salt
1 teaspoon sugar
2 teaspoons baking powder

½ teaspoon baking soda
8 tablespoons cold butter, cut into cubes
¾ cup buttermilk
1–2 tablespoons milk

Lois Wyse

Preheat oven to 450 degrees.

Sift dry ingredients together, and put into large mixing bowl. Cut in butter, one cube at a time, using a pastry cutter or two forks, until mixture is crumbly. Work in milk until soft dough forms.

Gather dough together and place on lightly floured board. Press with heel of hand into a large circle shape, about ½ inch thick. Using a 2½- to 3-inch biscuit or cookie cutter, cut out eight rounds and transfer to a cookie sheet, leaving one-inch space between each. Brush tops lightly with milk. Bake until golden and crisp, about 15 minutes.

Poulet Grandmere

This is about as French as a chicken recipe can get. Liza, who has spent much of her life in France, learned it from a neighborhood grandmother and, now that she is a grandmother herself, Liza likes making it even more. The important touch, Liza reminds us, is the addition of the big chunks of bacon.

MAKES 6 SERVINGS

1 pound slab bacon, cut into 1-inch dice
2 tablespoons butter
1 5-pound stewing or roasting chicken cut into serving pieces
1 large onion, chopped
2 leeks, white tops only, chopped
2 stalks celery with leafy tops, chopped
2 cloves garlic, minced
2 tablespoons flour
1 cup chicken stock
1 cup dry white wine
6 carrots, peeled and cut into 1-inch dice
4 boiling potatoes, peeled and cut into chunks
1 teaspoon salt
½ teaspoon dried thyme
1 bay leaf tied with 4 sprigs parsley
1 pound pearl onions, blanched and peeled
6 small white turnips, peeled and quartered

In small skillet, fry bacon until crisp. Drain on paper towel. Reserve bacon and 2 tablespoons fat.

In a large Dutch oven, heat butter and 2 tablespoons bacon fat. Add chicken and brown evenly. Remove and set aside.

Add onions, leeks, celery, and garlic. Sauté until softened, 3 to 4 minutes. Stir in flour, mix well, and cook 1 to 2 minutes more. Add stock and wine and mix well.

Return chicken to pot. Add carrots, potatoes, reserved bacon, salt, thyme, bay leaf and parsley. Bring liquid to a boil, cover pot, and braise in oven 1 hour. Add pearl onions and turnip, and continue braising another 30 minutes. Remove bay leaf and parsley package before serving.

Lois Wyse

Brunswick Stew

This recipe is as American as Betsy Ross and goes back to pre-Revolutionary days. It comes to us courtesy of our friend Patricia.

2 tablespoons vegetable oil
1 3–4 pound chicken, cut into serving
    pieces
1 large onion, chopped
2 pounds ripe tomatoes, peeled, seeded,
    and chopped
2 teaspoons sugar
1 cup boiling water or chicken stock
¼ teaspoon cayenne pepper
¼ teaspoon ground cloves
½ teaspoon salt
2 boiling potatoes, peeled and diced
3 cups fresh corn cut from the cob (about
    6 ears)
2 cups frozen lima beans
1 teaspoon Worcestershire sauce
1 tablespoon butter
1 cup fine bread crumbs
1 tablespoon fresh chopped parsley

In large pot, over high heat, heat oil and brown chicken evenly, 5 to 8 minutes. Stir in onion and cook until golden. Add tomatoes and sugar. Pour in water or stock, cayenne, cloves, and salt. Bring to boil, cover pot, and cook chicken over low heat, about 45 minutes.

Add potatoes, corn, beans, and Worcestershire sauce. Cook 10 minutes.

While stew is cooking the last 10 minutes, heat butter in small skillet, add bread crumbs, and toast lightly. Stir parsley into crumbs. Scatter crumbs over top of stew just before serving.

Chicken-and-Rice Casserole

(Arroz con Pollo)

Back in the days when everybody's mom stayed at home all day and neighbors were really neighbors, children visited back and forth in the kitchen next door—and children of different nationalities tasted the food in the neighbor's pot. That's the reason that Olga, Croatian by birth, knows this Spanish recipe. She still recalls the sight of sausages hanging in the kitchen of the Spanish family next door, sausages that went into the spicy *arroz con pollo* she was taught to make by a friendly, neighborly grandmother.

MAKES 8 SERVINGS

2 2–3 pound frying chickens, cut into serving pieces	*4 cups chicken stock*
salt and pepper to taste	*½ teaspoon saffron threads, crumbled*
4 tablespoons olive oil	*2 cups raw rice*
1 large onion, chopped	*1 pound fresh peas, shelled and cooked, or 1 10-ounce package frozen peas, thawed*
2–3 cloves garlic, minced	
4 ripe tomatoes, peeled, seeded, and coarsely chopped	*½ cup canned red pimento, diced (optional)*
1 teaspoon paprika	*2 tablespoons fresh chopped parsley*

Rinse chicken and pat dry with paper towel. Season with salt and pepper. Over high heat, heat oil in large pot or paella pan with lid, and brown chicken evenly on all sides. Remove from pan.

Stir in onions and garlic, and cook until soft. Stir in chopped tomatoes and paprika, and cook over low heat until mixture thickens and liquid evaporates, about 15 minutes. Put stock and saffron in saucepan, and bring to boil. Remove from heat, and set aside to soften saffron.

Stir rice into pot and mix well. Return chicken to pot and pour in hot stock. Reduce heat, cover, and simmer 20 to 30 minutes or until chicken is tender and rice has absorbed all liquid. Stir in peas, pimento, and parsley, and heat through.

Lois Wyse

Basque Chicken

Liza, who received this recipe from her French half sister, offers a grandmotherly hint in making this: be sure to remove all the pepper seeds. Cooked seeds are not only annoying but make the dish bitter.

MAKES 8 SERVINGS

1 3–4 pound chicken, cut into serving pieces
1 cup all-purpose flour
½ teaspoon salt
½ teaspoon freshly ground black pepper
½ teaspoon dried oregano
½ teaspoon dried marjoram
¼ teaspoon dried thyme
4 tablespoons olive oil
1 large onion, chopped
2 cloves garlic, minced
1 pound fresh mushrooms, trimmed and sliced

1 pound baked or boiled ham, diced
2 peppers, 1 green and 1 red, seeded and diced
4 ripe tomatoes, peeled, seeded, and diced
1 2-ounce can anchovy fillets, drained of oil and chopped
1 tablespoon tomato paste
1 cup dry white wine
1 pound Spanish chorizo sausage (or mild pepperoni), in 1-inch slices
2 tablespoons fresh chopped parsley

Rinse chicken and pat dry with paper towels. Mix flour with salt, pepper, oregano, and marjoram. Dredge chicken with seasoned flour. Over high heat, heat oil in large skillet and sauté chicken evenly. Remove and set aside.

Add more oil if needed, reduce heat to medium, and sauté onions, garlic, mushrooms, ham, and peppers until soft, about 8 to 10 minutes. Add tomatoes, anchovies, tomato paste, and wine. Bring to a boil. Return chicken to skillet. Cover, reduce heat, and simmer, about 30 minutes.

While chicken is cooking, fry sausage in separate skillet until brown and somewhat crisp. Add to chicken about 10 minutes before serving. Stir in parsley.

Chicken Cacciatore

When Rosemary, our Italian friend, gave us this recipe from her family, we thought it sounded familiar. It does, because this is one of those dishes that was made in every country, and given a name of its own.

MAKES 8 SERVINGS

2 2-pound frying chickens, cut into
    serving pieces
4 tablespoons each butter and olive oil
1 cup all-purpose flour
1 teaspoon dried oregano
1 teaspoon dried basil
½ teaspoon dried thyme
½ teaspoon salt
½ teaspoon freshly ground pepper
1 large onion, chopped
2 large leeks, whites only, chopped
3–4 cloves garlic, minced
1 pound fresh white mushrooms, trimmed
    and sliced

¼ cup brandy
3–4 pounds ripe tomatoes, peeled, seeded
    and chopped (or a 1-pound, 12-
    ounce can peeled Italian tomatoes,
    drained and chopped)
1 heaping tablespoon tomato paste
1 teaspoon sugar
½ cup dry white wine
1 bay leaf
2 tablespoons fresh lemon juice
2 tablespoons fresh chopped parsley

Preheat oven to 350 degrees.

Rinse chicken pieces and pat dry with paper towel. Heat butter and oil in deep skillet. Mix flour with oregano, basil, thyme, salt, and pepper. Dredge chicken in seasoned flour, shaking off excess. Brown evenly, and transfer to 4-quart glass casserole.

Add onions, garlic, leeks, and mushrooms to skillet and cook until golden, 5 to 8 minutes. Add brandy, bring to boil, and reduce liquid by half. Add tomatoes, paste, sugar, wine, and bay leaf. Boil, scraping up any bits from bottom of skillet.

Spoon sauce over chicken, cover with foil and bake, about 1 ½ hours. Remove bay leaf and stir in lemon juice and parsley just before serving.

Chicken and Cornbread Dressing

(Preacher's Sunday Night Supper)

If you were born in the South, you know this famous Sunday night supper. It combines fresh vegetables, leftovers and is a thrifty dish, an important consideration when the preacher was coming to supper, and folks didn't want to look too fancy. A preacher's daughter (who prefers to remain anonymous) learned this recipe from a parishioner.

MAKES 6 TO 8 SERVINGS

For the CORNBREAD DRESSING

1 teaspoon baking powder

½ teaspoon baking soda

1½ cups buttermilk

1½ cups yellow cornmeal

½ cup all-purpose flour

½ teaspoon salt

1 egg, lightly beaten

2 tablespoons melted shortening or bacon
    fat

6 strips bacon

4 tablespoons butter

1 onion, diced

2 stalks celery with leafy tops, chopped

1 green bell pepper, seeded and diced

2 tablespoons chopped fresh parsley

½ teaspoon dried thyme

salt and freshly ground black pepper to
    taste

¼ teaspoon paprika

1 cup chicken stock, heated

For the CHICKEN

1 5–6 pound roasting chicken

1 lemon

salt and freshly ground black pepper to
    taste

dash garlic powder

dash paprika

1 onion, halved and sliced

2–3 carrots, peeled and thickly sliced

2 stalks celery, sliced

2–3 sprigs fresh parsley

¼ teaspoon dried thyme

For the GRAVY

Reserved pan juices

1 tablespoon cornstarch

1 cup cold water

Salt and freshly ground black pepper to
    taste

continued on next page

To make the cornbread dressing:

Preheat oven to 475 degrees. Have ready a heavy, black iron skillet. Place skillet in heated oven.

Dissolve baking powder and soda in buttermilk. Mix cornmeal with flour and salt. Stir buttermilk mixture into cornmeal. Mix in egg. Carefully remove hot skillet from oven. Pour shortening into skillet, swirl until hot, then add to batter. Mix slightly, pour batter into skillet and return to oven. Reduce heat to 450 degrees and bake 15 to 20 minutes, until top crust forms. Remove from oven and allow to cool. When cornbread is cool, remove from skillet and crumble into bowl.

In small skillet, fry bacon until crisp, drain on paper towel, and chop. Discard all but 1 tablespoon bacon fat. Add 2 tablespoons of butter to bacon fat. Heat and sauté onion, celery, and green pepper over medium heat, 2 to 3 minutes. Add the parsley, thyme, salt, pepper, and paprika. Mix well. Stir in bacon bits and crumbled cornbread. Melt remaining 2 tablespoons of butter and stir into mixture, along with hot chicken stock. Mixture should be moist, but not too wet. If too dry, add more stock. Let mixture cool completely before stuffing chicken.

To make the chicken:

Preheat the oven to 400 degrees. Rinse chicken inside and out and pat dry with paper towel. Cut lemon in half and rub over chicken. Squeeze juice into cavity, then stuff with cooled dressing. Do not pack too tightly. Sew cavity closed or close with poultry skewers. Rub chicken with salt, pepper, garlic powder, and paprika. Scatter onion, carrots, celery, parsley, and thyme over bottom of pan. Place on rack in center of roasting pan, put chicken on rack, breast side up. Pour in 1 cup water or chicken stock and roast 30 minutes.

Reduce heat to 350 degrees and continue roasting another 1½ hours, or about 20 minutes per pound. Baste occasionally with pan juices, adding additional liquid if needed. When chicken is done, transfer to carving platter, cover with foil, and keep warm.

To make the gravy:

Dissolve 1 tablespoon cornstarch in 1 tablespoon of cold water and stir into pan juices. Bring mixture to boil. Stir well. Season with salt and pepper and strain. Pass hot gravy with chicken and stuffing.

Chicken Spaghetti

This is an Alabama version of spaghetti and meatballs. Estralita, a war bride who married a World War II soldier, came to Birmingham to make her home and, with this recipe, she added a little spice to Southern cooking.

MAKES 6 TO 8 SERVINGS

1 5–6 pound stewing hen
1 large onion, chopped
2–3 stalks celery, chopped
2–3 carrots, peeled and chopped
4 sprigs fresh parsley
1 bay leaf
1 teaspoon salt
½ teaspoon black pepper
2 tablespoons skimmed fat from broth, or
    2 tablespoons butter
2 large onions, chopped
4 stalks celery with top greens, chopped
1 large green bell pepper, seeded and
    chopped

½ pound fresh mushrooms, quartered (or
    canned mushrooms)
2–3 cloves garlic, minced
4 tablespoons chopped fresh parsley
1 6-ounce can tomato paste
1 1-pound, 14-ounce can chopped tomatoes
1 tablespoon Worcestershire sauce
½ teaspoon sugar
½ teaspoon red-pepper flakes or Tabasco
    sauce
1 pound spaghetti, cooked and drained
½ pound grated Parmesan cheese

Put hen in soup pot with onion, celery, carrots, parsley, bay leaf, salt, and pepper. Cover with cold water and bring to a boil. Reduce heat, cover, and simmer until hen is tender, about 2 hours. Remove and cool.

Skim fat from broth as it cools, and reserve. Strain broth and discard solids. Reserve broth. When hen is cool, remove meat, discarding skin and bones. Chop or shred meat and set aside.

Over high heat, heat 2 tablespoons of skimmed fat or butter in large pot. Sauté onions, celery, green pepper, mushrooms, and garlic a few minutes, until softened. Stir in parsley, tomato paste, tomatoes with liquid, and one cup of reserved broth. Bring to boil and cook until sauce thickens, about 15 minutes. Add Worcestershire, sugar, and pepper flakes or Tabasco. Sauce should be somewhat liquid, but not too thin.

Stir in chicken and spaghetti. Cook mixture about 20 minutes. If the mixture seems dry, add more broth. Just before serving, stir in cheese.

Chicken Egg Foo Yoong

No, this is not a recipe from a Chinese grandmother. It's an American-born grand-mother's idea of what exotic cookery was all about and was given to us by Sharon, a New York friend.

MAKES 8 SERVINGS

4–6 tablespoons peanut or vegetable oil
1 whole boneless and skinless chicken
    breast, cut into thin strips
1 small onion, diced
½ pound fresh white mushrooms, thinly
    sliced
½ cup water chestnuts, thinly sliced and
    halved

2 cups fresh or canned bean sprouts,
    rinsed and drained
2–3 scallions, chopped
2 tablespoons soy sauce
1 teaspoon salt
1 teaspoon sugar
8 eggs, beaten

For the **SAUCE**

1 cup chicken broth
2 teaspoons soy sauce
½ teaspoon salt

1 tablespoon cornstarch, dissolved in 2
    tablespoons cold water

Over high heat, heat 1 tablespoon oil in a skillet and stir-fry chicken 2 to 3 minutes. Add onions, mushrooms, and water chestnuts. Stir-fry another 1 to 2 minutes. Add bean sprouts and scallions, fry 1 minute. Add soy sauce, salt, and sugar, mix well, and set aside to cool. When cool, fold in beaten eggs. Set aside.

Heat 2 teaspoons oil in small frying pan until hot. Ladle in ⅛ of the egg mixture. Cook until eggs are set and browned on one side, turn over and brown on the other. Remove from skillet and continue this process until all mixture has been used. Add more oil with each pancake. Set pancakes aside while making sauce.

TO MAKE THE SAUCE:

Stir broth, soy sauce, salt, and cornstarch together in small saucepan and set over medium heat. Bring to a boil, whisking constantly, until sauce thickens. Serve hot sauce spooned over pancakes.

Lois Wyse

Chicken Paprikash

Grandmother Eva's secret for making this traditional Hungarian dish is to use plenty of sweet paprika. Another grandmotherly reminder: Add the sour cream at the very end, or you'll have a curdled mess.

MAKES 6 SERVINGS

2 2–3 pound frying chickens, cut into
  serving pieces
1 cup all-purpose flour
6 tablespoons oil or chicken fat
1 cup chicken stock
1 teaspoon salt
2 large onions, sliced into thin rings
2 large red bell peppers, seeded and sliced
  into thin rings
2 large green bell peppers, seeded and
  sliced into thin rings

4 ripe tomatoes, peeled, seeded, and
  chopped
4 tablespoons sweet
  Hungarian paprika
1 teaspoon sugar
½ teaspoon freshly
  ground black
  pepper
1 cup sour cream
2–3 tablespoons
  chopped fresh
  parsley, for garnish

Rinse chicken pieces and pat dry with paper towel. Dredge chicken in flour, shaking off excess.

Over high heat, heat 4 tablespoons oil in large pot, and brown chicken evenly. Add stock and salt, cover, reduce heat to low, and cook 1 hour. While chicken is cooking, heat remaining oil in large skillet and sauté onions and peppers, 1 to 2 minutes. Add tomatoes, paprika, sugar, and black pepper. Mix well. Spoon over chicken in pot and mix.

Cover, and continue cooking until chicken is tender, about 30 minutes. Transfer chicken to serving platter.

Remove pot from heat and stir in sour cream. Spoon sauce over chicken and serve, garnished with chopped parsley.

Chicken Fricassee with Parsley Dumplings

Dumplings are a grandmother dish if ever there was one. When Joan's grandmother gave us this recipe, she said to be sure to remind cooks that the trick in dumpling making is not to overboil; it's a tender touch that is needed here.

½ cup all-purpose flour
½ teaspoon salt
½ teaspoon dried thyme
¼ teaspoon black pepper
⅛ teaspoon cayenne pepper
1 4–5 pound stewing hen or roasting chicken, cut into serving pieces
4 tablespoons butter
4 tablespoons corn oil
1 large onion, chopped

2 carrots, peeled and diced
2 stalks celery, diced
1 bay leaf
2 cloves garlic, peeled
6 cups chicken stock
6 tablespoons all-purpose flour, dissolved in 6 tablespoons cold water
Parsley dumplings (recipe follows)

Mix flour with salt, thyme, and peppers. Rinse chicken and pat dry with paper towel. Dredge chicken with seasoned flour, shaking off excess.

Heat butter and oil in deep skillet until hot and foamy. Brown chicken until crispy, about 10 minutes. Remove from pan and set aside.

Add onion, carrots, and celery and sauté, about 5 minutes. Return chicken to pot with bay leaf, garlic cloves, and chicken stock. Bring to boil, reduce heat, cover, and simmer, about 1½ to 2 hours. Remove chicken from pot and set aside.

Discard bay leaf and garlic. Bring stock to boil, whisk in dissolved flour, and allow liquid to boil and thicken. Return chicken to pot and drop dumpling batter by spoonfuls on top of boiling liquid. Cover pot, reduce heat, and simmer until dumplings are tender, 12 to 15 minutes.

PARSLEY DUMPLINGS

2 ½ cups all-purpose flour

3 teaspoons baking powder

1 teaspoon sugar

½ teaspoon salt

3 tablespoons cold butter, cut into small bits

1 cup milk, or as needed

1 tablespoon chopped fresh parsley

Mix flour, baking powder, sugar, and salt in bowl. Using two forks or a pastry cutter, add butter in small pieces, a little at a time, until crumbly. Pour in milk and mix to form a soft dough that will drop easily from a spoon. Use a bit more milk if necessary. Mix in parsley.

Drop by spoonfuls onto simmering liquid.

Roast Duck with Red Cabbage and Spatzle

Grandmothers had a way with spatzle, but if you're worried that your spatzle won't come out tiny and separate like Grandma's, try the method described here. Sherri learned it works best. It's an old traditional way of making spatzle that gives you better control over the consistency.

MAKES 4 TO 6 SERVINGS

DUCK

2 4–5 pound ducks
1 teaspoon salt
½ teaspoon freshly ground black pepper
1 teaspoon mixed dried herbs (thyme, rosemary, marjoram)

1 onion, quartered
1 green apple, cored, peeled, and quartered

Preheat oven to 450 degrees.

Trim away all fat at base of tail and neck of each duck, and any excess fat or skin. Rub ducks inside and out with salt, pepper, and herbs. Put onion and apple pieces in cavities and place on rack in roasting pan.

Pour 1 cup boiling water into bottom of pan and roast 1 hour. Reduce heat to 400 degrees, and continue roasting until skin is crisp and brown, and breast juice runs clear when pierced with a sharp knife, about 1 hour more.

Transfer ducks to carving board and remove onion and apple pieces from cavities. Carve and serve with red cabbage and spatzle (recipes follow).

Lois Wyse

BRAISED RED CABBAGE
WITH CARAWAY

1 2-pound head red cabbage	½ teaspoon salt
1 tablespoon salt	¼ teaspoon freshly ground black pepper
2 teaspoons lemon juice	¼ cup apple-cider vinegar
¼ pound bacon, minced	2 tablespoons honey
1 onion, chopped	1 teaspoon cornstarch
2 tart apples, cored, peeled, and diced	¼ cup beef or chicken stock
½ teaspoon caraway seeds	

Cut cabbage in half, cut out and discard core. Shred cabbage and put into large bowl. Sprinkle with salt and let stand until juices run, about 15 minutes.

Have ready a pot of boiling water. Rinse cabbage and drain. Drop into pot and blanch, 1 to 2 minutes. Drain under cold water. Put in a bowl and sprinkle with lemon juice. Set aside.

In a small skillet, sauté bacon until crisp. Add onions and sauté until golden, 1 to 2 minutes. Add apples, caraway seeds, salt, pepper, vinegar, and honey. Mix well. Mix cornstarch in stock until dissolved. Stir into skillet and bring to a boil. Cook until clear, 1 to 2 minutes. Stir into cabbage. Transfer to large saucepan, cover, and cook over very low heat, stirring occasionally, about 1 hour. Add boiling water if liquid evaporates and cabbage seems dry. Taste for sweet-and-sour balance, and adjust vinegar and honey, if necessary.

continued on next page

SPATZLE

MAKES 4 TO 6 SERVINGS

4 eggs

3 cups all-purpose flour

½ teaspoon baking powder

1 teaspoon salt

1 cup milk

¼ teaspoon nutmeg

melted butter, for serving

fine breadcrumbs, for serving

Combine eggs, flour, baking powder, salt, milk, and nutmeg, and beat well with wooden spoon or electric mixer.

Bring large pot of salted water to a boil. Place dough on floured cutting board and press with heel of hand to about one-half-inch thickness. Hold board on an angle to lip of the pot. Gradually cut dough into strips or small pieces, and push carefully into the boiling water. Do this in batches, taking care not to overcrowd the pot or spatzle will stick together. Cook 6 to 8 minutes, removing with slotted spoon to a warm serving plate. Continue in this manner until all dough has been cooked. Drain well. Pour on a bit of melted butter and a tablespoon or two of fine breadcrumbs.

Lois Wyse

Sausage-and-Chestnut Dressing for Poultry

Here's a dressing for poultry that we like with turkey. So, why do we mention turkey in a chapter devoted mainly to chicken? Because a little boy we know told his grandmother, "Turkey is my favorite kind of chicken."

MAKES ABOUT 8 CUPS

1 pound sweet pork sausage, crumbled
2 tablespoons butter
1 1-pound can cooked chestnuts, chopped
1 onion, chopped
2 stalks celery with top greens, chopped
2 large tart, green apples, cored, peeled, and chopped

½ cup dried apricots, soaked in boiling water, drained, and diced
4 cups dried bread cubes
1 teaspoon salt
½ teaspoon ground black pepper
¼ teaspoon ground fennel
½ teaspoon ground sage
1 cup hot chicken stock

Sauté sausage in skillet until brown. Add butter and sauté chestnuts, onion, celery, apples, and apricots with sausage, mixing well, another 2 to 3 minutes.

Put bread cubes in large bowl and add skillet ingredients. Stir in salt, pepper, fennel, and sage, and mix well. Add hot stock, stirring to form a moist consistency. Add more stock, if necessary.

MEATS

YOU CAN RECOGNIZE HER AT THE AIRPORT, BE-
CAUSE SHE'S THE ONE WHOSE LUGGAGE CONSISTS
OF ONE TINY OVERNIGHT BAG AND SIX PAPER
shopping bags. She's the grandmother, of course, the one with a pot roast,
the Easter ham, the pirogis, and the Christmas cookies. She's the family
bag lady because, as they all assure her, "Mom, nobody makes it like you."

And probably nobody does.

Distance and time tend to flavor our memory.

Perhaps that is why Olga, who can't remember the name of her grandmother's
sausage dish, can still remember its aroma. "That aroma was my promise that on the back
burner of Grandma's stove there would be a pan sizzling with sautéed onions, garlic, very
ripe tomatoes, cabbage with pork chops, and Grandmother's own German sausage. No, I
can't name it," she confesses, "but some days I can still taste it."

Scottish grannies began the week with Sunday dinner and a traditional serving of
roast beef, Yorkshire pudding, and cauliflower. And then the thrifty grandmothers parceled
out leftovers to fill the week. Mondays meant cold roast beef and horseradish sauce; Tues-
day, housewives served chipped beef with stovers (sautéed potatoes); Wednesday, shepherd's pie or "mince with mash." If a housewife were lucky, Thursday she would still have
enough bones for stock—they would be used again on Friday and go on to become Saturday's
delicious soup. And on Sunday, she would use the drippings from the previous Sunday roast
for the Yorkshire pudding.

Anastasia remembers her grandmother soaking cabbage leaves in barrels of brine
for three days, then rolling them with ground pork to make her Greek stuffed cabbage—tell

that story of three days of preparation to a granddaughter who wants to microwave her present, past, and future foods.

On the other hand we might tell the story of the granddaughter who, when she made a pot roast, cut off one end. "Why?" asked her husband. "Because my grandmother did," she replied. Next time she spoke with her grandmother, the granddaughter asked Granny the reason. To make it cook faster? Slower? "No, no," Grandmother answered. "My pan was too small."

Elizabeth, who grew up in New Orleans, remembers that her grandmother arose at 5 A.M. and started her day's cooking by rotating huge iron pots on her stove. Even at breakfast, the smells of jambalaya, stews, and red beans and rice filled the air. "It was good," Elizabeth recalls, "but Grandma sure cooked the hell out of everything. In those days it was considered good cooking to overcook everything you made."

But lest you think all grandmothers were chained to the kitchen range, remember that at least one grandmother we know came out of the kitchen long enough to discover store-bought bread, called it her salvation, and never baked again. Her granddaughter, on the other hand, is known by her friends as the best bread baker in town.

You see, it's not just shirtsleeves to shirtsleeves in three generations—sometimes it's apron to apron.

MEATS

Meatloaf

Johnny Mazetti

Picadillo

Stuffed Cabbage

Boiled Meat Dinner (Cocido)

Braciolini

Beef Rouladen

Brisket of Beef

Pot Roast

Sauerbraten

Beef Stroganoff

Lamb Stew

Moussaka

Ham Croquettes with Onion Sauce

Cuban Pork Roast

Stuffed Pork Chops

Braised Veal Shanks (Osso Bucco)

Veal Stew (Blanquette de Veau)

Wiener Schnitzel

Roast Beef and Yorkshire Pudding

Shepherd's Pie

Meatloaf

What can we say about meatloaf? If you were a grandmother, you made it and then let the family choose the way to eat it. Some ate it hot from the oven, others cold from the refrigerator. Our friend Charlotte in Iowa loved it best as a leftover on good, thick bread and with plenty of mayonnaise. Who knew about cholesterol?

MAKES 8 SERVINGS

½ cup coarse fresh breadcrumbs	1 large egg, beaten
½ cup milk	½ cup cream
2 pounds ground chuck beef	½ teaspoon dried thyme
½ pound ground pork	½ teaspoon dried sage
½ pound ground veal	1 teaspoon salt
¼ pound ground pork sausage, optional	½ teaspoon freshly ground black pepper
1 medium onion, finely chopped	¼ teaspoon nutmeg
2 cloves garlic, minced	3 small pats unsalted butter
2 tablespoons chopped fresh parsley	

Preheat oven to 375 degrees.

Soak breadcrumbs in milk. Mix meats together in large bowl. Add onions, garlic, parsley, and soaked breadcrumbs. Mix well with hands.

Beat egg with cream. Add the egg mixture, thyme, sage, salt, pepper, and nutmeg. Use fingers to rake meat and allow air through mixture. Cover with wax paper and let rest 5 to 10 minutes.

Shape meat to fit ungreased 9- x 5- x 3-inch ovenproof loaf pan and transfer. Make three indentations evenly across top. Place small pat of butter in each impression. Cover with foil and bake 1 hour. Uncover and continue to bake until top is lightly brown and crisp, another 30 minutes.

Unmold loaf onto serving platter, reserving pan drippings for gravy (recipe follows). Keep warm in low oven while making gravy.

continued on next page

GRAVY

2 tablespoons pan drippings
1 tablespoon all-purpose flour
½ cup chicken or beef stock
½ cup tomato sauce

¼ teaspoon dried thyme
½ teaspoon salt
freshly ground black pepper
pinch of sugar

Put pan drippings into small saucepan and stir in flour until paste forms. Whisk in stock and tomato sauce, stirring well, and bring to boil. Season with thyme, salt, pepper, and sugar. Cook over medium heat until smooth.

Lois Wyse

Johnny Mazetti

If you remember this, you probably had a Southern grandmother, because kids in the South grew up with this yummy, meaty version of macaroni and cheese.

MAKES 8 SERVINGS

2 pounds ground chuck beef
2 onions, finely chopped
2 green peppers, seeded and chopped
2 stalks celery, chopped
1 8-ounce can sliced mushrooms with
    liquid
1 14-ounce can tomato sauce
1 10-ounce can tomato soup

½ cup pimento-stuffed olives, sliced
½ teaspoon salt
¼ teaspoon freshly ground black pepper
1 pound sharp cheddar cheese, grated
1 12-ounce package medium wide noodles
    or macaroni noodles, cooked and
    drained

Preheat oven to 350 degrees. Have ready a greased 3-quart casserole with lid.

In a large skillet, fry meat over low heat until it gives off some fat. Increase heat, and add onions, peppers, and celery. Continue to fry, breaking up large chunks of meat with back of spoon, until lightly browned. Add mushrooms, tomato sauce, tomato soup, olives, salt, and pepper. Mix well. Stir in cooked noodles and cheese. Transfer mixture to casserole. Bake 20 to 30 minutes.

Grandma Guadeloupe gave us this recipe. She also gave us her recipe for longevity: Each day she consumed half a grapefruit, a banana, and a small shot of "rock-and-rye."

MAKES 8 SERVINGS

1½ pounds ground beef
½ pound minced ham
1 large onion, chopped
1 green pepper, seeded and chopped
1 clove garlic, mashed
1 14-ounce can crushed tomatoes with
    liquid
1 teaspoon capers
¼ cup pimento-stuffed olives, chopped
1 tablespoon chopped fresh parsley

1 teaspoon salt
½ teaspoon freshly ground black pepper
½ teaspoon ground cumin
½ teaspoon red-pepper flakes
¼ teaspoon ground cloves
1 hard-cooked egg, chopped
fluffy rice, for serving
black beans, for serving
fried plantains (see page 129), for
    serving

In a large skillet over medium heat, sauté beef, breaking up large chunks with back of wooden spoon. When meat is browned, push to one side of skillet, and add ham, onion, green pepper, and garlic. Fry until golden, 3 to 5 minutes. Add the tomatoes and their liquid, capers, olives, parsley, salt, pepper, cumin, pepper flakes, cloves, and egg. Mix well. Continue cooking until all liquid has been absorbed, 8 to 10 minutes. Mixture should be moist. Serve with fluffy rice, black beans, and fried plantains.

Stuffed Cabbage

My grandmother, who made a lot of stuffed cabbage in her life, used to shake her head sadly whenever she cleared the table and saw the food her children and grandchildren left on their plates. "A sin," she would sigh. "It's a sin," and promptly ate all the leftovers. Years later she would admit, "I got fat on the sins of my children."

MAKES 6 TO 8 SERVINGS

1 large head green cabbage
2 pounds ground beef
½ cup raw rice
1 small onion, grated or finely diced
1 clove garlic, minced
1 teaspoon salt
½ teaspoon freshly ground black pepper
1 tablespoon chopped fresh parsley
1 egg

2 tablespoons vegetable oil
1 1-pound can sauerkraut, drained and rinsed
1 large onion, thinly sliced
1 cup sugar
1 1-pound, 14-ounce can crushed tomatoes
2 tablespoons lemon juice

Bring large pot of water to rolling boil. Put cabbage in pot, cover, simmer 10 minutes. Remove from pot, set aside to cool. Remove core and separate leaves. Set aside 12 large, whole leaves. Chop remaining cabbage. Reserve 2 cups of cabbage water and discard the rest.

Put meat, rice, onion, garlic, salt, pepper, and parsley in bowl and mix well. Mix in egg and ½ cup cabbage water. Place heaping spoonful of meat in center of each cabbage leaf. Fold leaf over meat, envelope style, tucking in sides.

Heat oil in large pot. Add sauerkraut, chopped cabbage, and onion. Sauté over low heat until cabbage softens, about 10 minutes.

Put sugar in small skillet and slowly brown sugar over very low heat until it turns pale golden, 3 to 5 minutes. Add sugar to pot along with tomatoes, remaining reserved cabbage water, and lemon juice. Season with additional salt and pepper.

Place rolls, seam side down, snugly in pot, spooning sauce up and over. Bring mixture to boil, reduce heat to simmer, cover pot, and cook 1 hour. Taste sauce for more sugar or lemon juice, if needed.

Joe remembers Sunday night dinners at his grandmother's house because she always served *cocido*, a Spanish version of the Italian *bollo misto*, and the French cassoulet. He knew the minute he walked into her house and took one whiff of the smoked meats and sauce that once again he would eat more than he should. But isn't that what makes a grandmother happy?

MAKES 6 TO 8 SERVINGS

2 pounds smoked pork tenderloin
1 pound beef chuck, or roast with bones in, or flanken
¼ pound salt pork
1 pound chickpeas, soaked overnight in cold water
3 pounds small boiling potatoes, peeled

3–4 large carrots, peeled and cut into chunks
4 Spanish chorizos or morcillas sausages
1 2-pound head green cabbage, cored and quartered
freshly ground black pepper, to taste

Have ready a soup pot filled with boiling water. Add meats and salt pork. The pot should be about three-quarters full of water, and the meats completely submerged. Add chickpeas, simmer 1½ hours. Add potatoes and sausage, continue simmering ½ hour. Add kale, simmer ½ hour more. Cool overnight.

Skim off fat and discard. Reheat. Adjust seasoning. First, serve bowls of broth, then follow with carved meat, sausage, and the vegetables.

Lois Wyse

Braciolini

There must be thousands of grandmothers who made *braciolini*, but it is Maria Renda's grandmother's recipe we used. Is it exactly like Grandma's? "No," Maria admits, "because even though I asked, she never did give me the recipe. But I watched her make this so many times that I think I memorized her movements. What makes this truly distinctive, I think, was Grandma's secret of adding a pat of butter in the center before rolling the meat."

MAKES 8 SERVINGS

2 pounds beef round cut into very thin
    slices
2 cups fresh breadcrumbs
1 cup grated Parmesan cheese
4 cloves garlic, mashed

2 teaspoons dried oregano
4 tablespoons
    chopped
    parsley
8–10 ounces butter

MARINADE

¼ cup red wine vinegar
½ cup olive oil

2 garlic cloves, mashed
1 teaspoon oregano

Using a mallet, pound the beef slices until flattened to ¼-inch thick. Combine breadcrumbs, cheese, garlic, oregano, and parsley and mix well. Spread mixture over each slice, and top with a knob of butter. Fold in sides and roll up to form little bundles. Secure with toothpick or thread bundles together onto a long skewer. Continue until all of the meat and stuffing has been used.

    Combine marinade ingredients. Place meat in a large glass dish with marinade, and refrigerate 2 to 4 hours.

    Preheat broiler, put skewers of meat on broiler pan or rack, brush with marinade, and broil 5 to 10 minutes, turning, until nicely browned. Remove from skewers to a warm platter and serve with pan juices.

Beef Rouladen

If you're thinking of going on a diet, forget about beef rouladen. But if you'd like a real taste of German cooking, try this one. Grandmother's hint: Be certain to use plenty of that good, hot, German mustard.

MAKES 8 SERVINGS

1 cup German-style Dusseldorf mustard
4 pounds top round of beef (cut into about 16 very thin 4-ounce slices)
8 strips bacon, cut in half
1 pound ground pork
1 large onion, finely chopped
4 dill pickles, cut vertically into 4 long, thin slices each
1 cup all-purpose flour

½ teaspoon salt
½ teaspoon freshly ground black pepper
3–4 tablespoons vegetable oil
½ cup dry red wine
1½ cups beef stock
2 teaspoons cornstarch dissolved in 1 tablespoon cold water
1 bay leaf
¼ teaspoon dried thyme

Spread 1 teaspoon mustard over each slice of meat. Top with a piece of bacon, and spread with a tablespoon of pork. Sprinkle with chopped onion and top with pickle slice. Carefully roll up each slice, tucking in sides, to form a cylinder. Secure end with toothpick or tie with string.

Mix flour with salt and pepper. Dredge rolls in seasoned flour, shaking off excess.

Heat oil in large skillet. Brown bundles, turning carefully, until evenly browned on all sides. Remove from skillet and set aside. Pour wine into skillet, bring to boil, scraping up any browned bits. Add stock, cornstarch, bay leaf, and thyme. Bring mixture to simmer, stir well, and return meat to skillet. Cover and simmer until meat is tender, 30 to 45 minutes.

Lois Wyse

Brisket of Beef

We know a couple of other ways to make brisket, but this recipe seems to be a grand-mother favorite. Some grandmothers using this recipe add an extra piece of flanken. We were told, however, of one grandmother-to-be who adds Grand Marnier and orange marmalade, plus an occasional mandarin orange to her brisket. It may not be her grand-mother's—but then whose grandma had access to packaged onion soup?

MAKES 8 SERVINGS

1 6-pound piece first cut brisket	¼ teaspoon dried rosemary
¼ cup red-wine vinegar	¼ teaspoon dried thyme
2 medium onions, chopped	1 bay leaf
2 green peppers, seeded and chopped	1 teaspoon salt
2 1-pound cans stewed tomatoes	½ teaspoon freshly ground black pepper
2 packages dried onion soup	dash red-pepper flakes

Trim excess fat from meat and place in roasting pan. Mix remaining ingredients and pour over meat. Cover pan tightly with foil and bake undisturbed for 2½ hours. Remove from oven, and thinly slice meat against the grain. Return meat to pot and braise another hour.

P̲o̲t̲ R̲oast

There are probably as many recipes (and variations) of pot roast as there are grand-mothers. So even if your grandma wasn't born a Yankee, she probably ended up, just like all of us grandmothers, making her version of Yankee pot roast.

MAKES 8 SERVINGS

*1 6–7 pound piece boneless beef rump or
    shoulder*
½ cup flour
1 teaspoon salt
½ teaspoon freshly ground black pepper
3 tablespoons vegetable oil
3 large onions, thinly sliced
2 cloves garlic, minced
2 bay leaves

½ teaspoon dried rosemary
½ teaspoon dried thyme
3–4 sprigs fresh parsley
2 cups dry red wine
2 cups beef stock
2 tablespoons Worcestershire sauce
*6 large carrots, peeled and cut into
    chunks*
mashed potatoes, for serving

Preheat oven to 350 degrees.

Mix flour with salt and pepper. Dredge meat in seasoned flour. Heat oil in large Dutch oven. Brown meat on all sides and remove. Add onions, sauté until golden, 3 to 4 minutes. Stir in garlic, and sauté 1 minute more. Add the bay leaves, rosemary, thyme, parsley, wine, and stock. Bring to boil. Stir in Worcestershire and return meat to pot. Cover, and bake 2 hours. Add carrots, and braise another 30 minutes.

To serve, remove meat and place pot on top of stove. Discard bay leaves and parsley sprigs. Bring liquid to rolling boil and reduce slightly. Slice meat against the grain.

Serve with mashed potatoes and pan juices.

Lois Wyse

Sauerbraten

Grandmother had her secrets. Some she shared, some she didn't. But this German grandmother was willing to tell her daughter that the secret to sauerbraten was gingersnap cookies. Surprised us, too.

MAKES 8 SERVINGS

½ cup dry red wine

½ cup red-wine vinegar

2 cups cold water

1 medium onion, thinly sliced

½ teaspoon whole peppercorns

3–4 whole cloves

4 whole juniper berries, crushed and
    flattened with edge of knife or
    mortar and pestle

2 bay leaves

1 teaspoon salt

2 carrots, peeled and sliced

4–5 pound piece
    boneless rump
    roast or top round

3–4 tablespoons lard
    or vegetable oil

1 large onion, finely
    chopped

2–3 large carrots, peeled and finely
    chopped

2 stalks celery, finely chopped

2 tablespoons all-purpose flour

1 cup beef stock

½ cup crushed gingersnap cookies

In a large saucepan, combine wine, vinegar, water, onion, peppercorns, cloves, juniper berries, bay leaves, salt, and carrots. Bring mixture to boil and cook 5 minutes. Remove from heat and allow to cool.

Trim fat from meat and put into a deep glass dish. Pour on cooled marinade. Cover dish with plastic wrap and refrigerate for 2 days, turning meat occasionally.

Remove meat from marinade and pat dry with paper towels. Strain marinade and reserve. In large Dutch oven, over medium heat, heat fat and brown meat evenly on all sides until deep golden brown. Remove meat, and set aside. Add chopped onions, carrots, and celery, and cook over medium heat for 5 to 8 minutes. Sprinkle flour over vegetables, stir well to incorporate, and cook 2 to 3 minutes, until flour turns golden. Whisk in 2 cups of reserved

continued on next page

Sauerbraten (cont.)

marinade and the stock. Bring to boil, reduce heat, and return meat to pot. Cover and simmer, over low heat, for 2 to 3 hours, or until meat is fork tender. Transfer meat to platter and keep warm in low oven.

Skim fat off top of pan juices, and transfer juices to saucepan. Reduce juices over high heat to 2½ cups. Lower heat to medium, stir in gingersnaps, and simmer for 10 minutes or until sauce begins to thicken. Strain through sieve, pressing hard on solids to extract all juices. Discard solids. Slice meat thin and serve with sauce.

Lois Wyse

Beef Stroganoff

Today's grandmothers remember beef stroganoff, not because they learned the recipe from their grandmothers, but because it was the number-one party dish of the 1950s suburban housewife. Nobody claimed to be a czarina, but everyone felt positively royal when she put her silver chafing dish (a wedding gift) on the dining room table (paid for slowly, very slowly), and waited for guests to ooh and aah over her special recipe.

MAKES 4 SERVINGS

1 pound boneless beef (flank steak, sirloin, or tenderloin)
1 tablespoon butter
1 tablespoon vegetable oil
1 medium onion, thinly sliced
½ pound fresh mushrooms, trimmed and thinly sliced

2 teaspoons cornstarch, diluted in 1 tablespoon cold water
½ cup beef stock
Salt and pepper to taste
½ cup sour cream
1 teaspoon Dijon mustard
buttered noodles for serving

Trim fat from meat and cut across grain into thin slices. Heat butter and oil in large skillet. Add meat and cook, stirring, until lightly browned, 2 to 3 minutes. Remove meat from pan, add more fat if needed.

Sauté onions and mushrooms 2 to 3 minutes until golden. Return meat to pan and mix well. Stir cornstarch mixture into stock and whisk into skillet. Season with salt and pepper and bring to a boil for 1 to 2 minutes.

Remove from heat, stir in sour cream and mustard. Serve immediately with buttered noodles.

Lamb Stew

Although this recipe calls for new potatoes, it can also be made with large chunks of boiling potatoes. Liza remembers mashing the potatoes and turnips together while eating her grandmother's (and mother's) stew.

MAKES 8 SERVINGS

4–5 pounds boneless lamb shoulder or shoulder chops	1 teaspoon dried rosemary
1 cup flour	1 teaspoon dried thyme
1 teaspoon salt	2 bay leaves
½ teaspoon freshly ground black pepper	16 small new potatoes, peeled
4 tablespoons vegetable oil	8 small white turnips, peeled and quartered
4 tablespoons butter	8 carrots, peeled and cut into chunks
2 tablespoons sugar	24 baby pearl onions, blanched and peeled
2 tablespoons tomato paste	1 10-ounce box frozen green peas, defrosted
3–4 cups beef stock	1 pound fresh green beans, trimmed, cut into pieces, and blanched
3 ripe tomatoes, peeled, seeded, and chopped	
2 cloves garlic, minced	

Preheat oven to 350 degrees.

Trim excess fat from lamb and cut into 2-inch cubes. If using chops, leave whole.

Mix flour with salt and pepper. Dredge meat with seasoned flour, shaking off excess. Over high heat, heat oil and butter in Dutch oven, and lightly brown meat on all sides. When all meat has been browned, sprinkle sugar over all, and toss to caramelize. Stir tomato paste into stock and mix well. Add to pot along with tomatoes, garlic, rosemary, thyme, and bay leaves. Cover and cook in oven 1 hour.

Add potatoes, turnips, and carrots and continue braising 30 minutes. Add onions, and bake another 15 to 20 minutes, until meat is fork tender and potatoes are done. Scatter peas and beans over top, and finish cooking a final 10 to 15 minutes. Remove bay leaves before serving.

Lois Wyse

Moussaka

The Greeks had a word for it—and it is *moussaka*. This recipe comes from an extraordinary Greek cook, and the special secret is to follow the recipe step-by-step and remember to salt the eggplant to draw off any bitterness.

MAKES 8 SERVINGS

3 medium eggplants, sliced ½-inch thick
1 tablespoon coarse kosher salt
1 cup plus 2 tablespoons all-purpose
    flour
3–4 tablespoons olive oil
½ pound ground beef
½ pound ground lamb
2 large onions, finely chopped
½ pound fresh white mushrooms, trimmed
    and thinly sliced
2–3 cloves garlic, minced
1 14-ounce can crushed tomatoes
1 8-ounce can tomato puree
2 tablespoons tomato paste

1 teaspoon dried basil
1 teaspoon dried oregano
½ teaspoon dried thyme
2 bay leaves
1½ teaspoons salt
½ teaspoon freshly ground black pepper
1 teaspoon ground cinnamon
1 cup dry red wine
2 tablespoons butter
2 cups milk
¼ teaspoon white pepper
dash ground nutmeg
1 egg yolk, lightly beaten
grated Parmesan cheese

Preheat oven to 375 degrees.

Lay slices of eggplant out on flat surface. Sprinkle with coarse salt and let stand 30 minutes. Rinse slices and pat dry with paper towel. Dredge in 1 cup flour and shake off excess.

Over medium heat, heat oil in large skillet. Lightly brown eggplant, about 2 minutes on each side. Remove from pan and drain on paper towel. Add more oil, if needed, and put beef and lamb in skillet. Brown meat, breaking up large chunks with back of wooden spoon. Push meat to one side, add onions and mushrooms and sauté about 5 minutes until golden. Add garlic, tomatoes, puree, paste, basil, oregano, thyme, bay leaves, 1 teaspoon salt, pepper, and cinnamon. Mix well. Pour in red wine. Bring to boil, and stir over medium heat until liquid has evaporated and sauce is thick. Set aside to cool.

continued on next page

Over medium heat, melt butter in saucepan and whisk in 2 tablespoons flour, stirring to form a roux. Whisk in milk slowly, cook until sauce thickens. Season with ½ teaspoon salt, white pepper, and nutmeg. Remove from heat. Put a tablespoon of sauce into egg yolk and mix well. Return egg mixture to sauce and mix. Cover with plastic wrap and set aside.

Place a layer of eggplant on bottom of 9- x 13-inch glass ovenproof dish, cover with some meat sauce, and alternate layers until all eggplant and sauce have been used. Cover entire top with white sauce and sprinkle with Parmesan cheese. Bake I hour.

NOTE: *All lamb may be used, if desired.*

Lois Wyse

Ham Croquettes with Onion Sauce

This is about as English a recipe as one can get. Annie remembers her grandmother's big old Aga stove with all the children sitting 'round after school to keep warm. "We drank milky tea and waited 'til it was time for Grandmother to begin making our ham croquettes."

MAKES 6 TO 8 SERVINGS

3 tablespoons butter
4 tablespoons all-purpose flour
1 cup milk
dash salt
dash white pepper
dash nutmeg
1 egg yolk, lightly beaten
2 cups finely minced cooked ham
2 scallions, trimmed and finely minced
1 tablespoon grated onion

1 tablespoon chopped fresh parsley
½ teaspoon salt
¼ teaspoon freshly ground black pepper
¼ teaspoon paprika
1–2 cups fine dry breadcrumbs
2 eggs, lightly beaten with 2 tablespoons
    cold water
fat for deep frying
Onion Sauce (recipe follows)

Melt butter in saucepan until foamy. Whisk in flour, stirring to form a roux. Slowly whisk in milk, bring mixture to boil, season with salt, pepper, and nutmeg. Cook over low heat 2 to 3 minutes. Remove from heat, put a tablespoon of sauce into egg yolk, mix well, and return egg mixture to sauce. Add ham, scallions, onion, parsley, salt, pepper, and paprika. Mixture should be very thick.

Spread mixture out on plate, cover with plastic wrap, and chill thoroughly.

Heat a deep fryer to 375 degrees. Form mixture into cones or balls. Roll in breadcrumbs, dip in beaten egg, then in crumbs again. Drop into hot fat, and fry 3 to 5 minutes until golden and crisp. Remove with slotted spoon and drain on paper towel. Serve with onion sauce.

continued on next page

Just Like Grandma Used to Make . . .

ONION SAUCE

MAKES 2 CUPS

4 tablespoons butter

1 medium onion, minced

2 shallots, finely minced

2 leeks (whites only), minced

2 tablespoons all-purpose flour

2 cups chicken stock

½ teaspoon salt

¼ teaspoon white pepper

2 teaspoons fresh snipped chives

Melt butter in saucepan. Sauté onion, shallots, and leeks for 15 minutes over very low heat until golden. Stir in flour, whisk in stock, and bring to boil. Add salt and pepper, reduce heat, and simmer about 5 minutes until sauce is thick. Spoon over croquettes and garnish with chives.

Lois Wyse

Cuban Pork Roast

When Juanita came to the United States, she brought her great-grandmother's ring—and her grandmother's recipe. This Cuban pork roast, like many good Cuban dishes, combines sweetness with a spicy note.

MAKES 8 SERVINGS

1 5-pound boneless loin of pork
½ cup orange juice
1 fresh lime, juiced
3 cloves garlic, minced
2 teaspoons dried oregano
½ teaspoon dried sage
¼ teaspoon ground ginger

1 tablespoon olive oil
½ teaspoon salt
¼ teaspoon freshly ground
    black pepper
1 onion, chopped
1 carrot, chopped
2 stalks celery, chopped

Preheat oven to 325 degrees. Pat meat dry with paper towel. Put in glass dish. Mix orange and lime juice together, pour over meat, and marinate several hours. Remove meat from dish, reserving marinade.

Mix garlic, oregano, sage, ginger, olive oil, salt, and pepper, and rub over meat. Scatter chopped onion, carrot, and celery over bottom of shallow roasting pan, and place meat on top. Pour reserved marinade into roaster. Roast meat, uncovered, about 2½ hours, or until internal temperature of meat reaches 175 degrees, basting often. Add more juice if liquids evaporate.

Remove meat from pan, place on ovenproof platter, and return to low oven to keep warm. Pour pan juices into saucepan, bring to a boil, and reduce slightly, about 10 minutes. Skim fat, and serve with sliced meat.

Stuffed Pork Chops

Grandmothers have always been quick to add something new to something old. These stuffed pork chops prove that a grandmother will figure a way to stuff anything—this time the pork chops are stuffed with apples. Well, that's a grandmother for you.

Makes 8 servings

8 loin pork chops (1½ inches thick), with
    pockets for stuffing
salt, pepper, and paprika to taste
6 tablespoons butter
¼ cup minced ham
½ pound fresh white mushrooms, finely
    minced
1 small onion, finely chopped
1 small tart apple, cored, peeled, and
    finely chopped

1 tablespoon dried currants
½ cup coarse fresh breadcrumbs
2 tablespoons chicken stock
½ teaspoon dried tarragon
1 tablespoon chopped fresh parsley
1 cup all-purpose flour
½ cup chicken stock
½ cup white wine

Preheat oven to 350 degrees.

Season pork chops with salt, pepper, and paprika, and set aside.

In a large skillet, heat 3 tablespoons of butter, and sauté ham, mushrooms, onion, apple, and currants until soft and golden, about 5 minutes. Add breadcrumbs, stock, tarragon, and parsley. Mix well to form a soft stuffing. Cool to room temperature.

Put a small amount of stuffing into pocket of each chop. Close with toothpick. Dredge chops in flour, shaking off excess. Heat remaining butter in skillet, and sauté chops on each side, about 3 to 4 minutes. Transfer to shallow 9- x 13-inch glass ovenproof dish, pour in stock and wine, cover with foil, and bake 20 minutes. Uncover and bake until tops are brown, 15 to 20 minutes.

Lois Wyse

Braised Veal Shanks
(Osso Bucco)

Isabella came from Italy with a set of her grandmother's marrow spoons. She thought she would need them in America, but try as she might, she never found any use except to scoop the marrow from her own osso bucco, better known here as braised veal shanks. Isabella did tell us, however, how to add that last fillip to the dish—be sure to look for it in the recipe.

MAKES 8 SERVINGS

5 pounds veal shanks, cut into 2–3 inch
    pieces
salt and freshly ground black pepper to
    taste
1 cup all-purpose flour
4 tablespoons olive oil
2 carrots, finely diced
2 onions, finely diced
2 stalks celery, finely diced
3 cloves garlic, minced

1 cup dry white wine
1 cup beef stock
3 ripe tomatoes, peeled, seeded, and
    chopped
1 tablespoon tomato paste
½ teaspoon dried rosemary
½ teaspoon dried basil
¼ teaspoon dried thyme
1 bay leaf
2 navel oranges

GREMOLATA

grated rind of 1 lemon
2 tablespoons chopped fresh parsley

1 clove garlic, minced

Mix all the gremolata ingredients together. Set aside until serving time.

Preheat oven to 350 degrees. Pat meat dry with paper towels, and season with salt and pepper. Dredge in flour, shaking off excess.

Heat oil in Dutch oven, and brown meat evenly on all sides. Remove meat from pot. Add more oil if needed.

continued on next page

Sauté carrots, onions, celery, and garlic over medium heat until golden, about 5 minutes. Pour in wine and stock, bring to boil, and scrape up browned bits. Return meat to pot. Add tomatoes, tomato paste, rosemary, basil, thyme, and bay leaf. Cut rind from oranges in long thin strips and julienne. Set aside. Juice oranges and add juice to pot. Cover and braise 2 hours, or until meat is fork-tender.

While meat is cooking, put orange rind strips in small saucepan. Cover with cold water and bring to boil. Simmer 5 minutes, drain, and rinse with cold water. Set aside. Stir into pot about 15 minutes before meat is done. Remove bay leaf.

Stir *gremolata* into meat juices just before serving.

Lois Wyse

Veal Stew
(Blanquette de Veau)

In France this is classic farmhouse food. Rafaela, who lives in Paris, gave us this recipe because, as she cautioned, "You can't have a grandmother's cookery book without blanquette."

MAKES 8 SERVINGS

5 pounds boneless veal, cut into 2-inch cubes

salt and freshly ground black pepper to taste

4 tablespoons butter

6 large leeks, whites only, well-washed and thinly sliced

6 shallots, chopped

2 cloves garlic, minced

½ cup all-purpose flour

1 cup dry white wine

1–2 cups chicken stock

2 stalks celery

4 sprigs fresh parsley

2 sprigs fresh dill

2 bay leaves

4–5 carrots, peeled and sliced

½ pound pearl onions, blanched and peeled

½ cup heavy cream

2 tablespoons fresh lemon juice

2 tablespoons fresh chopped dill

Preheat oven to 350 degrees.

Rub veal with salt and pepper. Heat butter in Dutch oven. Brown veal over medium heat, 7 to 8 minutes. Add leeks, shallots, and garlic. Cook 5 minutes more. Sprinkle with flour, stir to combine, and cook 2 to 3 minutes. Pour in wine, scraping up browned bits from bottom. Boil for 2 to 3 minutes, and add enough stock to almost cover meat.

Tie celery with parsley, dill, and bay leaves. Add celery bundle to pot. Cover, put in oven, and braise 1 hour. Add carrots and continue braising until meat is fork tender, about 1 hour. Stir in pearl onions 10 minutes before meat is done.

Remove from oven; discard celery bundle. Stir in cream. Heat through. Stir in lemon juice and dill. Season with salt, pepper, and a dash of nutmeg.

Wiener Schnitzel

This goes back to Vienna and a grandmother's real comfort food. When the egg was added on top, it was considered a special child's treat. Adults loved it, too, but Grandmother always said, "I'm doing it for the *kinder* (children)."

MAKES 6 TO 8 SERVINGS

1 cup all-purpose flour

1 teaspoon salt, divided

1 teaspoon freshly ground black pepper, divided

2 cups finely grated breadcrumbs

½ teaspoon paprika

3 pounds boneless veal cutlets (about 16 slices) pounded thin

4 eggs, lightly beaten with 2 tablespoons cold water

8 tablespoons butter

2 lemons, each cut into 8 slices

2 cans rolled anchovies with capers, well drained (optional)

2 tablespoons chopped fresh parsley

Preheat oven to 200 degrees.

Mix flour with ½ teaspoon salt and ½ teaspoon pepper in shallow pie plate. Mix breadcrumbs with ½ teaspoon salt, ½ teaspoon pepper, and paprika in another shallow pie plate. Dip veal in flour, shaking off excess. Dip in beaten eggs, then breadcrumbs. Press crumbs firmly onto meat. Place meat on cookie sheets in one layer. Allow to rest at room temperature 1 hour.

In large skillet, over high heat, heat 2 tablespoons butter. Sauté veal slices, turning carefully, until golden brown and crisp, about 3 minutes on each side. Continue adding butter and meat until all has been sautéed. Keep cutlets warm in oven.

Garnish each with lemon slice, a rolled anchovy in center of slice, and chopped parsley.

A fried egg on top of each slice of veal turns this dish into Veal à la Holstein.

Lois Wyse

Roast Beef and Yorkshire Pudding

There is nothing more British (unless it's the Beefeaters or Buckingham Palace) than roast beef and Yorkshire pudding. It's as much a staple in the English family as steak and potatoes in the United States. This recipe comes from generations of grandmothers.

MAKES 8 SERVINGS

1 7–8 pound rib roast of beef (about 4 ribs)
salt and freshly ground black pepper to taste
2 tablespoons Dijon mustard

1 small onion
1 tablespoon all-purpose flour
2 cups beef stock
Yorkshire pudding (recipe follows)

Preheat oven to 450 degrees.

Trim some fat from top of roast and season roast with salt and pepper. Rub mustard over all and score fat. Place meat, fat side up, in shallow roasting pan. The ribs will act as a rack. Place in oven and roast 30 minutes. Reduce oven to 350 degrees and continue to roast to desired doneness: 15 minutes per pound for rare, 18 minutes for medium, and 20 minutes for well done. Baste often with pan juices.

Remove meat from oven when done and allow to rest 15 minutes before carving. Reserve 4 tablespoons of fat from roasting pan for Yorkshire Pudding.

Put pan on top of stove. Add onion, sauté in drippings, 2 minutes. Add flour and cook, stirring, 2 to 3 minutes. Pour in stock and scrape up browned bits from bottom. Continue cooking over low heat until mixture boils and thickens. Strain into small saucepan and keep warm over low heat. Season with salt and pepper. Cut meat away from bones and slice thin. Cut bones apart if desired and serve. Serve with gravy and Yorkshire pudding.

continued on next page

Just Like Grandma Used to Make . . .

YORKSHIRE PUDDING

1 cup all-purpose flour
½ teaspoon salt
2 eggs, lightly beaten

2 cups milk
4 tablespoons pan drippings

Preheat oven to 425 degrees.

Sift flour with salt into a bowl. Make a well and drop in eggs. Gradually pour in half the milk and begin stirring, pulling in flour from sides of bowl. Beat well. Whisk in remaining milk. Cover and allow to stand, at room temperature, 30 minutes. Pour drippings into 9-x-13 inch glass ovenproof dish. Heat in oven until fat is very hot. Pour batter from bowl into hot fat and bake until puffy and brown, 25 to 30 minutes.

Individual puddings can also be made in 12 muffin tins filled ⅔ full and baked for 15 to 20 minutes.

Lois Wyse

Shepherd's Pie

Jane's grandmother always had a meat grinder affixed to the kitchen table in order to grind leftover roast beef for this English dish, which is traditionally made with lamb. But Jane's grandmother was an innovative cook. Still, when food processors became popular, she never settled for anything but her own hand-grinding. To clean the grinder, Grandmother put a piece of bread through the blades.

MAKES 8 SERVINGS

2 pounds boiling potatoes

4 tablespoons butter

¼ cup milk, heated

salt and freshly ground black pepper to taste

2 pounds fresh ground or leftover roast beef, finely minced

2 onions, finely chopped

2 carrots, peeled and finely chopped

2 stalks celery, finely chopped

2 tablespoons chopped fresh parsley

½ cup leftover roast beef gravy or beef stock

1 tablespoon Worcestershire sauce

½ teaspoon salt

¼ teaspoon freshly ground black pepper

Preheat oven to 400 degrees. Grease a 9- x 13-inch ovenproof glass dish.

Put potatoes in pot, cover with cold water, and cook 20 minutes, until very tender. Drain and mash until smooth, adding 2 tablespoons of the butter and the milk. Season with salt and pepper. Set aside.

In large skillet, over medium heat, heat remaining butter. Sauté meat, onions, carrots, and celery 5 to 8 minutes, until soft and golden. Stir in parsley, gravy or stock, Worcestershire sauce, and salt and pepper. Mix well. Spoon into dish, cover with mashed potatoes, and bake until brown and bubbly, about 35 to 40 minutes.

NOODLES, GRAINS, AND RICE

IF GOD GAVE YOU A JEWISH OR ITALIAN GRAND-
MOTHER, THEN VEGETABLES ARE SPELLED
N-O-O-D-L-E-S OR P-A-S-T-A.

Rice and dumplings, noodles and pasta, are not just accompa-
niments; they are often the foods that characterize a "grandmother"
dinner.

Sherri remembers Grandma Bertha, who made her own noodles every Friday for
Sabbath dinner. Some of those noodles became the main attraction in the chicken soup, others were the base of noodle pudding. Grandma's trick was to make the noodles early enough
in the day so that they might be stretched and laid to dry while the children were at school.
She liked to use the dining room table since it was big, stood in the middle of the room, and
could be circled with ease (despite her bulk). Grandma would stretch a clean bedsheet over
the table, roll and cut her noodles and drape them like the fringe of a scarf over the table to
dry. Then, just before the children came home from school, Grandma would gather her perfect noodles over her arm and march triumphantly into the kitchen to finish her soup and
make her pudding.

Other grandmothers had their secret ways of making a specialty. One, known for
the unusual shape of her dumplings, rolled and cut her dough into different shapes, quietly
wrapped each piece around her arthritic index finger, and presto! Unique shapes for
Granny's dumplings.

See why some grandmother secrets can't be duplicated?

NOODLES, GRAINS, AND RICE

Noodle Pudding

Spaghetti with Cauliflower and Zucchini

Macaroni 'n' Cheese Casserole

Lasagna

Kasha with Bowtie Noodles

Toasted Barley Pilaf

Hushpuppies

Fluffy White Rice with Fried Plantains

Italian Rice Balls (Arancine)

Dirty Rice

Red Beans and Rice (Washday Supper)

Chinese Fried Rice

Noodle Pudding

There are as many variations of noodle pudding as there are grandmothers. Some grandmothers add pineapple, some make noodle pudding with raisins. Other grandmotherly additions include nuts, cinnamon, orange marmalade, and, for a savory pudding, mushrooms and herbs. This recipe is the good, old-fashioned, basic recipe with sour cream—the one preferred by Sherri, our resident expert on the subject.

MAKES 12 TO 15 SQUARES

1 pound extra-wide noodles, cooked and drained	2 cups sour cream
8 tablespoons butter	6 extra-large eggs, separated
2 cups small-curd cottage cheese	½ teaspoon salt

Preheat oven to 375 degrees.

Put noodles into large mixing bowl and add butter, one tablespoon at a time, to hot noodles, allowing butter to melt. Mix in cottage cheese and sour cream. Add yolks to noodles with a pinch of salt. Mix well. In a separate bowl, whip whites until thick but not stiff. Fold into noodles.

Pour noodle mixture into 9- x 13-inch ovenproof glass baking dish, and bake in middle of the oven until lightly browned, about 1 hour. Cut into squares and serve.

VARIATION:

To make sweet noodle pudding, use unsalted (sweet) butter and add after the egg yolks:

2 tablespoons sugar	¼ teaspoon nutmeg
½ cup raisins	½ teaspoon vanilla
1 teaspoon cinnamon	

Proceed with recipe.

Lois Wyse

Spaghetti with Cauliflower and Zucchini

Anchovies let you know that this is a southern Italian dish—and as Liza learned during the years she lived in Europe, one *never* confuses southern Italian cooking with northern Italian cooking.

MAKES 6 TO 8 SERVINGS

3 tablespoons butter
½ cup dry breadcrumbs
½ cup olive oil
6 cloves garlic, chopped
4 medium onions, thinly sliced
1 large head cauliflower (2 pounds), trimmed and cut into florets
2 medium zucchini, sliced into ½" circles
salt and freshly ground black pepper
2 cups chicken broth

1 pound spaghetti
6 small ripe tomatoes, peeled, seeded, and chopped (canned may be substituted)
1 teaspoon anchovy paste
1 teaspoon red-pepper flakes, crushed
4 tablespoons chopped Italian parsley
¼ cup grated Parmesan or Romano cheese
salt and pepper

Melt butter in medium skillet over medium heat. Add breadcrumbs and sauté until lightly golden, 3 to 5 minutes. Set aside.

Over medium heat, heat ¼ cup olive oil in large skillet and sauté garlic, onions, and cauliflower until golden, about 5 minutes. Set aside. Add remaining oil and brown zucchini lightly, about 5 minutes. Season with salt and pepper. Remove and reserve with cauliflower. Add chicken broth to skillet. Bring to a boil and reduce liquid by half.

In a large pot, bring 6 quarts of water to a boil. Add pasta and cook until barely tender or *al dente*, 8 to 10 minutes. Drain.

While spaghetti is cooking, continue sauce. Add tomatoes and anchovy paste to broth and cook over medium heat, about 2 minutes. Add cauliflower, zucchini, and red-pepper flakes. If mixture seems dry, add more broth. Season with salt and pepper and simmer 5 minutes. Toss spaghetti with sauce, chopped parsley, and cheese. Top with toasted breadcrumbs and serve immediately.

Macaroni 'n' Cheese Casserole

We know that you could walk into any supermarket or convenience store and *buy* macaroni and cheese. But you'd never see a child's face light up the same way it would for the homemade version. So here's the old-time, all-time, classic recipe from Grandmother Florence who grew up on this very same recipe in Tulsa, Oklahoma.

MAKES 4 SERVINGS

1 pound elbow macaroni, cooked and
    drained
3 tablespoons butter
2 tablespoons all-purpose flour
2 cups milk
salt and freshly ground black pepper to
    taste

dash nutmeg
1 cup grated cheese (a combination of
    mild cheddar and processed
    American)
2–3 tablespoons dry breadcrumbs

Preheat oven to 350 degrees. Have ready a buttered 6-cup ovenproof glass baking dish.

Melt 2 tablespoons butter in saucepan and whisk in flour, stirring to form a paste. Do not brown. Whisk in milk and seasonings and bring to a boil, whisking constantly to prevent lumps. Reduce heat to simmer. Stir in grated cheese and cook over low heat until cheese is melted and mixture is smooth.

Fold sauce into macaroni. Turn mixture into baking dish. Melt remaining tablespoon butter in small skillet and add breadcrumbs. Toss crumbs, over medium heat, until lightly toasted. Add more butter, if needed. Sprinkle crumbs evenly over top of macaroni. Bake until the top is brown and bubbly, 15 to 20 minutes.

Lois Wyse

Lasagna

This is a dish that has wings. It flies, it drives, it goes wherever you take it. Lasagna is everyone's favorite, regardless of nationality, because the simmering flavors marry well and please children's palates as well as those of adults. Giuseppe remembers both his grandmothers making their sauce all through the day and, as the sauce bubbled in the pot, each grandmother would take a piece of homemade bread and dunk it in the sauce. Too much seasoning? Too little? Grandma knew!

MAKES 8 TO 12 SERVINGS

1 pound lasagna noodles, cooked and drained
1½ cups shredded mozzarella
2 cups fresh ricotta

⅔ cup finely grated Parmesan cheese
8 cups meat sauce (recipe follows) or marinara or tomato sauce

Preheat oven to 350 degrees.

Spread a thin layer of sauce into 10- x 14-inch ovenproof dish. Cover with a single layer of noodles, top with sauce, ricotta, mozzarella, and Parmesan. Continue layering until all pasta is used, ending with a layer of mozzarella and Parmesan. Bake 45 minutes.

MEAT SAUCE

2 tablespoons olive oil
1½ pounds ground beef
1 onion, finely chopped
3 cloves garlic, mashed
½ pound mushrooms, finely chopped
1 28-ounce can crushed plum tomatoes
1 cup tomato puree

1 6-ounce can tomato paste
½ teaspoon dried basil
½ teaspoon dried oregano
¼ teaspoon thyme
1 teaspoon sugar
1 tablespoon salt

In a large skillet, over high heat, heat 1 tablespoon of oil and fry ground meat, stirring to crumble. Drain and reserve meat. Heat remaining oil and sauté onions to soften. Add garlic and mushrooms, stir, cook 2 minutes over medium heat. Add the tomatoes, tomato puree, tomato paste, basil, oregano, thyme, sugar, and salt, and bring to a boil. Lower heat, cover, and simmer 20 minutes. Uncover and cook 20 minutes.

Kasha with Bowtie Noodles

The new emphasis on healthy eating has made kasha, also known as buckwheat groats, a new star in the health foods stores. The original, however, is a staple of Eastern European kitchens, and is translated here by Liza after trying a few friends' old favorites.

MAKES 8 SERVINGS

1 cup coarse kasha
1 large egg, lightly beaten
2 tablespoons butter (or chicken fat)
1 large onion, chopped
1 pound (4–5 cups) fresh mushrooms,
  sliced

1 teaspoon salt
1 teaspoon freshly ground black pepper
2 cups boiling chicken stock
2 cups bow-tie noodles, cooked and
  drained

Mix kasha and egg. Over high heat, heat a skillet, add kasha mixture, and cook, stirring, until mixture is dry and lightly toasted, about 5 minutes. Set kasha aside. Reduce heat to medium. Add butter and sauté onions and mushrooms until golden, about 8 minutes. Return kasha to skillet. Add the salt, pepper, and chicken stock, and cook, stirring frequently, until all liquid has been absorbed and kasha is tender, about 30 minutes. Stir in noodles and heat through.

Toasted Barley Pilaf

Barley is one of the best-tasting grains. Our friend Pauline gave us this recipe from her Polish grandmother.

1 cup pearl barley
½ cup dried mushrooms, preferably
    Polish, soaked in 1 cup boiling water
2 tablespoons butter (or chicken fat)
1 large onion, finely chopped
1 green pepper, seeded and diced

1 cup hot chicken stock
salt and freshly ground black pepper to
    taste
1 tablespoon finely chopped fresh parsley
1 tablespoon minced fresh dill

Heat a heavy skillet. Pour in barley and spread evenly over the bottom. Allow grain to toast but not burn. Stir frequently. Pour into bowl and set aside.

Drain mushrooms, squeeze out any excess liquid, and finely chop.

Preheat oven to 350 degrees. Over high heat, heat butter in skillet and sauté onions, peppers, and mushrooms until onions are golden, about 3 to 4 minutes. Stir in barley. Reduce heat to low, and pour in stock. Simmer on top of the stove, checking occasionally and adding additional ¼ cup of stock, if needed, or, transfer to a 2-quart casserole and bake 1 hour, stirring occasionally. Add salt and pepper and stir in parsley and dill before serving.

Hushpuppies

Here is another version of Southern fritters, this time made with cornmeal. Our recipe comes from Priscilla, the descendant of a South Carolina family, who tells us that tradition insists that hushpuppies be served with barbecue.

MAKES ABOUT 2 DOZEN

shortening or cooking oil for deep-fat
    frying
½ cup sifted all-purpose flour
1½ cups yellow cornmeal
2 teaspoons baking powder

1 teaspoon salt
1 medium onion, finely chopped
¾ cup milk
1 egg, beaten

Heat fat in deep fryer to 375 degrees.

Sift together flour, cornmeal, baking powder, and salt. Stir onion into flour mixture. Blend in milk and egg.

Drop teaspoons of batter into hot fat. Fry until golden brown, 3 to 5 minutes. Hushpuppies will float when they are done.

Drain on paper towels. Serve hot.

Lois Wyse

Fluffy White Rice with Fried Plantains

In case your grandmother never told you, remember that when cooking rice, you must use a pot with a tight-fitting lid. And no peeking! You have to let the rice do its work unobserved. A Colombian grandmother gave us this recipe. Plantains (which look like bananas but don't taste like them) can be combined with rice to make an excellent side dish and accompaniment to meats.

MAKES 8 SERVINGS

2 teaspoons butter or vegetable oil	1 teaspoon salt
2 cups long grain white rice (not converted)	Fried Plantains (recipe follows)

Choose a medium saucepan with a tight-fitting lid. Melt butter, add rice and cook, over medium heat, stirring constantly, until opaque, about 2 minutes. Add 3 cups of water, and salt, and bring to a boil. Stir.

Reduce heat to simmer. Cover saucepan with foil and lid to fit very tightly. Simmer until all the water has been absorbed, about 15 minutes. Turn off heat. Leave pan to rest another 15 minutes. Do not remove lid. Fluff the rice with a fork just before serving. Serve with plantains.

FRIED PLANTAINS

4 ripe plantains, peeled	½ cup vegetable oil

Cut plantains into long strips. Over high heat, heat oil in skillet, and fry slices until golden brown. Drain on paper towels before serving.

Italian Rice Balls
(Arancine)

It's hard to believe but, sometimes, there is leftover risotto. When that happens, this is the best possible recipe for rice balls. They are popular in central Italy and the south of Italy: Roman ones are made with red rice stuffed with meat and shaped like a croquette, while in Naples the rice balls are made with white rice and peas and are egg-shaped. Mariarita still makes her southern-style rice balls whenever her great-nephew comes to visit, and Darcy's grandmother manages to FedEx her rice balls to the Holy Land to relatives for Christmas.

MAKES 10 TO 12 RICE BALLS

1½ cups uncooked arborio or other short-grain rice, not converted
1 teaspoon salt
3 tablespoons olive oil
½ pound lean ground beef
¼ pound lean ground pork
1 teaspoon tomato paste
1 teaspoon dried basil
salt and freshly ground black pepper
¼ cup grated Parmesan cheese
3 eggs, beaten well
1 cup dry breadcrumbs
2–3 cups vegetable oil
½ cup chopped fresh Italian parsley

Bring two quarts of water to a boil in a saucepan and add rice and salt. Stir and bring back to a boil. Lower heat, cover, and simmer about 15 minutes. Drain.

While rice is cooking, heat olive oil in a skillet and add the meats. Cook over medium heat about 3 minutes. Add tomato paste with a teaspoon of water, basil, salt, and pepper. Continue to cook, stirring constantly, until thick, about 8 minutes. Remove from heat and stir in cheese. Mix well. Transfer to a plate to cool.

Lois Wyse

Put eggs in a shallow bowl. Put breadcrumbs in another shallow bowl. Have a bowl of warm water for dipping hands before shaping rice balls. Take a heaping tablespoon of warm rice and place in palm of hand. Using thumb, make a deep indentation in the rice ball. Spoon in 1 tablespoon of meat. Cover the filling with another tablespoon of rice. Press both hands firmly around rice to completely enclose the filling and form a firm ball. Roll balls in egg to coat, then in breadcrumbs. Place balls on cookie sheet lined with wax paper. Refrigerate 1 hour before frying.

Heat oil in a deep skillet or fryer to 350 degrees. Fry balls 3 at a time until golden on all sides. Drain on paper towel. They can be kept warm a few minutes in an oven set at 250 degrees. Pile up on a platter and sprinkle with chopped parsley. Serve immediately.

These are delicious served with warm tomato sauce.

Dirty Rice

When Betty Lou was a little girl, she used to go to her grandmother's house in the Garden District of New Orleans any time Granny made dirty rice. It's that recipe which has been passed on to us.

MAKES 8 SERVINGS

2 tablespoons butter
1 medium onion, finely chopped
1 red bell pepper, seeded and diced
1 green pepper, seeded and diced
2 cloves of garlic, mashed
1 stalk celery , diced
1 pound chicken giblets, diced
½ pound smoked ham, diced
2 cups long-grain white rice, not
    converted

1 teaspoon white pepper
1 teaspoon salt
½ teaspoon cayenne pepper
1 teaspoon dried oregano
1 bay leaf
freshly ground black pepper, to taste
1 teaspoon paprika
½ teaspoon dried thyme
4 cups boiling water or chicken stock

Over medium heat, heat butter in a deep large pot. Add onion, peppers, garlic, and celery and sauté until golden but not browned. Add giblets and ham and cook, stirring, 2 to 3 minutes more. Stir in rice and the white pepper, salt, cayenne, oregano, bay leaf, black pepper, paprika, and thyme. Mix well, and add more fat, if necessary. Pour in half the stock or water. Reduce heat to low. Simmer 10 minutes. Add remaining liquid and leave to simmer until all the liquid has absorbed. Fluff rice with a fork and remove bay leaf before serving.

Lois Wyse

Red Beans and Rice
(Washday Supper)

All the Mondays of Matt's childhood centered around Grandma's washday. On that day Grandma had no time to cook so she put a pot on the stove early in the day, let it simmer and, by the time the menfolk were ready to eat, so were the red beans and rice. Matt can't recall anyone ever eating red beans and rice in Alabama on any day but Monday.

MAKES 8 SERVINGS

2 pounds dried kidney beans, soaked overnight in cold water, drained
2 medium onions, chopped
1 green pepper, seeded and chopped
2 tablespoons finely chopped fresh parsley
2 cloves garlic, finely minced
1 pound smoked ham, diced
1 ham hock

1 teaspoon salt
½ teaspoon freshly ground black pepper
¼ teaspoon cayenne
2 bay leaves
½ teaspoon dried thyme
3 quarts water
6 andouille or Polish sausages, sliced
fluffy white rice, for serving (page 129)

Put all the ingredients except sausage in a heavy 8- to 10-quart pot. Bring to a boil, lower heat, and simmer 2 to 2½ hours, or until beans are tender. Stir from time to time, and scrape the sides and bottom of pot to prevent sticking. Add more water towards end of the cooking if beans seem dry.

In heavy skillet, fry sausages until brown and crisp on both sides, about 10 minutes. Drain. Add to beans for last 30 minutes of cooking. Remove ham hock and bay leaves before serving. Serve over fluffy white rice.

Chinese Fried Rice

If you're a fan of Chinese takeout, you know about Chinese fried rice. Or at least you think you do. Until you've made Chinese fried rice the authentic way, you've missed a very special treat. Mai Lin, a Chinese friend, gave this recipe to us.

MAKES 6 TO 8 SERVINGS

3 cups long-grain rice, cooked a day in advance
6 tablespoons peanut oil
1 medium onion, chopped
1–2 carrots, diced
¾ pound green beans, cut into ½-inch lengths
¾ cup frozen green peas, defrosted
1 6-ounce can bamboo shoots, sliced
4 large eggs, beaten with 1 teaspoon water

½ pound Chinese sausage or baked ham, chopped
¾ pound medium peeled shrimp, chopped, optional
salt and freshly ground black pepper, to taste
¼ cup soy sauce
4–6 scallions, chopped

Put cooked rice in large bowl.

Heat 2 tablespoons of oil in wok. Stir-fry onions and carrots, 2 minutes. Add beans and peas and stir-fry 2 minutes. Add bamboo shoots, and stir-fry I minute. Add to rice.

In a separate skillet, heat I tablespoon of oil, pour in eggs, cook until lightly browned. Flip over to brown on the other side. Remove to a chopping board and slice into thin slices. Add to rice.

In wok, heat I tablespoon oil. Stir-fry sausage or ham I minute, add shrimp, and cook until shrimp become opaque. Add to rice.

Heat remaining 2 tablespoons oil in wok and add rice mixture. Stir-fry, toss, and add salt, pepper, and soy sauce. Add scallions. Continue to toss and fry, I minute. Serve immediately.

Lois Wyse

VEGETABLES, BEANS, AND POTATOES

SK ANY AMERICAN GRANDMOTHER, AND CHANCES ARE HER FAMILY HAS STORIES OF THE VICTORY GARDEN THEY TENDED DURING WORLD WAR II. FOR MOST Americans, that was a time of shortages and inconveniences compounded by the constant concern for men and women in the armed forces, for families separated, and for lives put on hold. In the Victory Garden a large variety of vegetables was grown and, for many city dwellers, it was a first-time experience with the productivity of the land when well-tended.

Over the years, there has been a continuing emphasis on home-grown vegetables and that, coupled with our focus on fitness and health, has made vegetables earn a new and special place in Grandmother's recipe box.

We have come from the wartime days of: "Use it up, wear it out, make it do, or do without" to a generation that thinks it's cool to be a vegetarian and looks for innovative ways to make vegetables the center of the meal.

For those who want the newest in vegetables, it always pays to look back and see how Grandmother did it. Oh, those grandmas. They did know a thing or two about what's good for you!

Vegetables, Beans, and Potatoes

Baked Stuffed Artichokes

Glazed Acorn Squash

Brussels Sprouts with Bacon

Sweet-and-Spicy Beets

Hungarian Braised Cabbage

Carnabeet (Sephardic Casserole)

Carrot-and-Potato Casserole (Bombine Grand-Maman)

Glazed Sweet-and-Sour Carrots

Corn Pudding

Baked Beans

Hoppin' John

Creamed Spinach

Peas with Pearl Onions

Bashed Neeps

Potato Pancakes with Pink Applesauce (Latkes)

Mashed Potatoes

Scalloped Potatoes

Sweet Potato Casserole

Green Beans and Tomatoes

Stuffed Summer Squash au Gratin

Eggplant Parmesan

Chickpeas and Eggplant

Baked Stuffed Artichokes

Artichokes are a wonderful vegetable that Italian and Spanish grandmothers prepare regularly, but it is a vegetable that often frightens people—which part of the leaves to eat? Which to discard? In preparing artichokes Liza's grandmother trick is to remove the fuzzy "choke" with a serrated spoon.

MAKES 8 SERVINGS

8 medium artichokes	¼ teaspoon thyme
1 lemon, cut in half	2 cups fine dry breadcrumbs
½ cup olive oil	½ cup grated Parmesan cheese, plus
1 medium onion, finely chopped	additional for garnish
½ pound mushrooms, finely chopped	1 tablespoon tomato paste
2–3 cloves of garlic, mashed	2 tablespoons white wine
6 anchovy fillets (or 1 can), drained,	salt and freshly ground black pepper to
rinsed, and mashed	taste
2 tablespoons Italian parsley, chopped	8 ounces pitted black olives, chopped
½ teaspoon oregano	2 tablespoons capers
½ teaspoon basil	½ cup dry white wine
¼ teaspoon marjoram	½ cup chicken stock

TO COOK THE ARTICHOKES:

Trim stem flush with bottom of artichoke so that it will stand upright. Trim away any small tough leaves near bottom. Cut ½ inch off top, and use scissors to trim off sharp points on leaves. Immediately rub artichokes with lemon to prevent discoloration.

In large pot, arrange artichokes upright in 1 inch of boiling salted water. Cover and simmer until leaves pull off easily, and heart is tender when tested with a knife, about 20 minutes. Run under cold water and leave to drain, upside down on a rack, until cool enough to touch. Pull out center purple-tipped leaves. Then use a small spoon to scrape out all the hairy fuzz to expose the "heart" of the artichoke.

continued on next page

To make the stuffing:

Preheat oven to 350 degrees. Have ready 9- x 13-inch ovenproof glass baking dish. Heat olive oil in skillet and sauté onion, mushrooms, garlic, anchovies, and parsley, oregano, basil, marjoram, and thyme, until soft and golden. Stir in breadcrumbs, cheese, tomato paste, white wine, salt, and pepper. Remove from heat. Stir in olives and capers.

Spoon stuffing into the center of artichokes. Push additional stuffing down and around leaves. Place in baking dish and pour dry white wine and stock in and over artichokes. Drizzle with olive oil and additional grated Parmesan cheese. Cover dish with aluminum foil. Bake 20 minutes. Remove foil, bake an additional 10 minutes or until tops are crisp and brown.

Glazed Acorn Squash

This American recipe is for a dish that was often served at early Thanksgiving dinners. It works, however, at any time of year because squash is generally available—and very good.

MAKES 8 SERVINGS

4 medium acorn squash, cut in half
¼ cup orange juice, diluted with ¼ cup
    water
1 tablespoon honey

dash of allspice
1 cup cranberry sauce, homemade or
    canned

Preheat oven to 350 degrees.

Scrape seeds out of squash and, if necessary, cut a thin slice from bottom of squash so they stand upright. Pour orange juice into a 9- x 13-inch ovenproof glass dish and arrange squash cavity-side down in liquid. Bake until almost tender, about 30 minutes. Turn over, brush with honey, and sprinkle with allspice. Fill each cavity with 2 tablespoons of cranberry sauce. Bake an additional 15 minutes before serving.

Brussels Sprouts with Bacon

Anna remembers her grandmother in Belgium, who grew her own Brussels sprouts and cut them from a thick stalk with a heavy knife. But, as we turn back to the old and make it new again, our friend Anna reports that recently she went to a farmers' market and found Brussels sprouts still attached to their thick stalk.

MAKES 8 SERVINGS

½ pound bacon, cut crosswise into ½"
    strips
1 medium onion, sliced thinly
2 pounds Brussels sprouts, stems
    trimmed, tough outer leaves removed
½ cup water or chicken stock

2 teaspoons dried chervil or 2
    tablespoons chopped fresh parsley
salt and freshly ground black pepper to
    taste
3 tablespoons butter
1 cup dry breadcrumbs

Over medium heat, sauté bacon in large skillet until fat is rendered and bacon browns, about 10 minutes. Remove all but 2 tablespoons of bacon fat, and add onion and Brussels sprouts. Stir and cook over medium heat, about 5 minutes. Add water or chicken stock, bring to a boil, and cover. Lower to medium heat, and cook until sprouts are tender, about 15 minutes. Mix in chervil, season with salt and pepper.

Over medium heat, melt butter in skillet and add breadcrumbs. Stir until crumbs are toasted. Sprinkle crumbs over sprouts with additional parsley, if desired.

Lois Wyse

Sweet-and-Spicy Beets

The beet is one of the world's cheapest and most common of all root vegetables. This particular recipe sounds like a holiday dish but, in reality, grandmothers served it with simple boiled meats to give a lift to the taste buds.

MAKES 6 TO 8 SERVINGS

2 cups cooked beets, chopped
½ cup onions, thinly sliced
¼ cup orange juice, diluted with ½ cup
    water
juice of ½ lemon

¼ teaspoon cinnamon
¼ teaspoon nutmeg
salt and freshly ground black pepper
2 tablespoons unsalted butter

Preheat oven to 325 degrees. Have ready greased 1-quart baking dish.

Place beets and onions in dish. Add remaining ingredients and dot with butter. Cover with foil. Bake 1 hour.

Hungarian Braised Cabbage

Sonia still has her grandmother's pot, the one she used to make cabbage. Sometimes Grandmother kept a pot only for cabbage because, in the olden days, pots often played host to the cooked food odors long after dinner. One hint to keep a stove sweet-smelling and dispel cooking odors (remember, Grandmother didn't have a kitchen fan) was to put a small dish of vinegar in back of the burners.

MAKES 8 SERVINGS

3 tablespoons butter or bacon drippings	1 teaspoon caraway seeds
1 tablespoon onion, minced	dash nutmeg
1 large head white cabbage, about 3 pounds, shredded	salt and freshly ground black pepper to taste
1 cup sour cream, room temperature	

Over medium heat, melt butter in a large pan, and sauté onion until tender, about 10 minutes. Add cabbage and cook, stirring occasionally, until softened and liquid is absorbed, 15 to 20 minutes. Add sour cream, caraway seeds, nutmeg, salt, and pepper. Mix well. Serve warm.

Lois Wyse

Carnabeet

(Sephardic Casserole)

No, there are no beets in *carnabeet,* which is a Sephardic word for a vegetable casserole. Liza was given this recipe by her sister-in-law, who found it in an old-country cookbook.

MAKES 6 TO 8 SERVINGS

2 tablespoons vegetable oil
1 onion, finely chopped
1 medium head cauliflower, core removed,
    cut into florets
1 stalk celery, finely chopped
2 carrots, peeled and sliced
2 tomatoes, peeled, seeded, and chopped
½ pound green beans, trimmed and cut
    into ½-inch pieces
dash cayenne pepper
½ cup chicken stock
salt and freshly ground black pepper to
    taste

Over medium heat, heat oil in medium skillet, and sauté onion until tender, 8 to 10 minutes. Add remaining ingredients. Stir, cover, and simmer over low heat until vegetables are very tender, about 30 minutes. Add a little water during cooking time, if necessary. Season with salt and pepper before serving.

Carrot-and-Potato Casserole

(Bombine Grand-Maman)

Marie Josette, a grandmother in Provence, offered us her favorite recipe, and once you try it—who knows? It may be yours as well.

MAKES 6 TO 8 SERVINGS

4 tablespoons olive oil

1½ pounds onions, peeled and sliced

4½ pounds potatoes, peeled and cut into chunks

1½ pounds carrots, peeled and cut into chunks

½ teaspoon thyme

2 bay leaves

salt and freshly ground black pepper to taste

Over medium heat, heat oil in large pot, and sauté onions until softened, 8 to 10 minutes. Add potatoes, carrots, thyme, bay leaves, salt, pepper, and 1½ cups of water, and bring to a boil. Reduce heat, cover, and cook until water has evaporated, about 30 minutes. Vegetables should be slightly mushy. Adjust seasoning, and drizzle with additional olive oil, if desired.

Lois Wyse

Glazed Sweet-and-Sour Carrots

W ho says kids won't eat carrots? Grandma knew how to give carrots her own sweet touch, so that children wouldn't turn up their noses at vegetables. This recipe is glazed in my family memory.

MAKES 6 TO 8 SERVINGS

2 pounds carrots, peeled, trimmed, sliced
    diagonally about ¼-inch thick
3 tablespoons butter
2 tablespoons sugar or honey
¾ cup orange juice

1 tablespoon fresh lemon juice
salt and freshly ground black pepper to
    taste
chopped fresh parsley, for garnish

Put carrots, butter, sugar or honey, and orange juice in a nonreactive pot. Cover, and bring to a boil. Reduce heat and cook about 10 minutes. Uncover and cook until all liquid has been absorbed. Season with lemon juice. Add salt and pepper to taste. Sprinkle with chopped fresh parsley before serving.

Corn Pudding

Here's a recipe that goes back to the early American settlers. Our foremothers knew that the best way to make corn pudding was to get all the family to help scrape the corn off the cob. Tina, a grandmother in Bangor, tells us that this is still a good job for grandchildren!

MAKES 6 TO 8 SERVINGS

4 ears fresh corn or 2 cups canned or
    frozen corn
2 large eggs
1 cup milk
1 tablespoon sugar

½ teaspoon salt
¼ teaspoon freshly ground black pepper
dash cayenne pepper
1 tablespoon butter, softened
2 tablespoons fine fresh breadcrumbs

Preheat oven to 350 degrees. Butter a 1-quart casserole.

Use a sharp knife to scrape kernels from cob. Mix the corn, eggs, milk, sugar, salt, peppers, butter, and breadcrumbs together in a bowl and beat well. Pour into casserole, and bake until set, about 40 minutes.

Lois Wyse

Baked Beans

Our Boston grandmothers made the baked bean a national vegetable. It was a mainstay of Saturday night supper in many New England households.

1½ pounds white beans (such as navy beans or Great Northern beans)

½ pound sliced bacon, diced

1 medium onion, finely chopped

½ cup molasses

½ cup brown sugar

2 tablespoons prepared mustard

1 tablespoon cider vinegar

1 cup ketchup

salt and freshly ground black pepper

Soak beans overnight in cold water. Drain.

Preheat oven to 250 degrees.

In a skillet, sauté bacon until browned. Add onion, and continue cooking until onion has softened.

Put beans in Dutch oven, and add water to cover by 3 inches. Bring to a boil. Reduce heat and simmer ½ hour.

Stir bacon and onion into beans. Mix the molasses, sugar, mustard, vinegar, and ketchup together, and add to bean pot. Season with salt and pepper. Cover and place in oven for about 6 to 8 hours. Check beans hourly, and add more water if needed. Cook until beans are very tender.

NOTE: *Beans may also be simmered very slowly on top of the stove.*

Hoppin' John

Ginny from Georgia gave us her grandmother's old family recipe. Give it a try. It could become a new family favorite for you.

MAKES 6 TO 8 SERVINGS

6 slices bacon
4 stalks celery, chopped
1 large onion, chopped
½ pound fresh okra, sliced (or frozen)
1 14-ounce can diced tomatoes

2 cups cooked white rice
1 10-ounce package frozen black-eyed peas, defrosted
Tabasco sauce, for serving
Worcestershire sauce, for serving

In a skillet, cook bacon over medium heat until crisp. Drain on paper towels.

Reserve 2 tablespoons bacon drippings. Crumble bacon and set aside. In skillet, heat bacon drippings, and sauté celery and onion until softened, 2 to 3 minutes. Add okra, and continue cooking over medium heat another 10 minutes.

Stir in tomatoes and their juice, along with rice and black-eyed peas. Simmer until liquid is absorbed, about 3 minutes. Sprinkle top with crumbled bacon and serve with Tabasco and Worcestershire sauces.

Lois Wyse

Creamed Spinach

Spinach was no easy vegetable in Grandmother's day. She had to take the thick stalks, cut them, and then wash the spinach carefully, because it was full of sand and grit. One Italian grandmother solved spinach washing by cleaning out her laundry tubs, filling them with five pounds of spinach and carefully doing the spinach wash. Granddaughters have it a lot easier. We find spinach prewashed in groceries.

MAKES 6 TO 8 SERVINGS

6 pounds fresh, prewashed spinach

1 tablespoon butter

1 medium onion, finely chopped

for the SAUCE:

4 tablespoons butter

4 tablespoons all-purpose flour

1½–2 cups half-and-half or cream,
    heated

dash grated nutmeg

salt and freshly ground black pepper to
    taste

Wash spinach carefully in several changes of water to remove any sand or grit. Trim stems and discard tough outer leaves. Drain and chop.

Heat 1 tablespoon of butter in a large pot and sauté onion, 1 minute. Add spinach. Cover and cook over medium heat, 2–3 minutes. Stir and continue to cook until wilted and tender, about 4 minutes. Transfer to colander, drain, and squeeze out any excess moisture by pushing down hard with the back of a large spoon.

PREPARE SAUCE:

In medium saucepan heat butter until foaming. Stir in flour and cook over medium heat, 1 to 2 minutes. Whisk in hot cream. Continue whisking to remove lumps, until sauce becomes thick and smooth, about 5 minutes. Stir spinach into cream sauce. Season with a dash nutmeg, salt, and pepper before serving.

Peas with Pearl Onions

Often, a child's first experience with vegetables is peas. Here is a grown-up version from Paulette, a French grandmother.

MAKES 6 TO 8 SERVINGS

3 tablespoons butter

3 pounds fresh shelled green peas or 2 9-ounce boxes frozen

1 pound fresh pearl onions, blanched and peeled, or 1 10-ounce bag of frozen onions

6 leaves Boston lettuce, shredded

2 tablespoons chopped fresh parsley

¼ teaspoon chervil

1 tablespoon sugar

½ teaspoon salt

¼ cup chicken stock (water may be substituted)

Melt butter in saucepan and add remaining ingredients. Bring to a boil. Reduce heat, cover, and simmer until peas are tender, about 15 minutes.

NOTE: *If using frozen peas and onions reduce cooking time by half.*

Lois Wyse

Bashed Neeps

This is a Scottish dish that made its way across the sea. Teresa remembers her country grandmother coming to visit the family in the Illinois town of Winnetka, which she thought of as The Big City. Grandmother found the supermarket a treasure trove. Wide-eyed, she walked slowly up and down the aisles until she finally stopped in front of a bin filled with turnips. "Land sakes," she bellowed, "don't this just beat all! Turnips in a bag. These folks up here in Winnetka have to pay for turnips."

MAKES 8 SERVINGS

2 pounds rutabagas, peeled and cubed
1 pound potatoes, peeled and cubed
4–5 tablespoons butter

¼ teaspoon freshly grated nutmeg
salt and freshly ground black pepper to taste

Add rutabaga to a large pot of salted, boiling water and cook 10 minutes. Add potatoes and cook until fork-tender, about 15 minutes. Drain and return vegetables to pot with butter. Mash until smooth and season with nutmeg, salt, and pepper. Reheat over very low flame. Adjust seasoning before serving.

Potato Pancakes with Pink Applesauce

(Latkes)

No Chanukah celebration is complete without latkes and applesauce. Every child can remember grating potatoes until knuckles were raw, but as every grandmother knows, they're not potato pancakes if they're made with a mix. Potato pancakes and applesauce are also a favorite Sunday night supper at Sherri's home.

MAKES 45 TO 50 4-INCH PANCAKES

8–10 pounds Idaho potatoes, peeled
4 large Spanish onions, peeled and cut in
    half
4 cloves garlic, minced (optional)
12 large eggs
1 one-pound box matzo meal
    (approximately 2 cups)

2 teaspoons salt
2 teaspoons baking powder
3 cups pink applesauce (recipe follows),
    for serving
2 cups sour cream, for serving

Grate potatoes on a hand grater or use grating blade of food processor. Do not overprocess—the potatoes must have texture. Grate onions into potatoes and transfer to large mixing bowl. Add garlic if desired. Stir in eggs, enough matzo meal to thicken, salt, and baking powder. Mixture should not be too liquid. Mix well.

In large skillet, heat I inch vegetable oil. Drop in batter one tablespoonful at a time, making latkes as large (or small) as desired.

Use fork and spoon to turn latkes as they fry. Remove from skillet when golden-brown and crisp. Drain on cookie sheet lined with paper towels. Try to stand the latkes in rows on their ends; the oil will drain off more efficiently.

Keep warm in low oven (250 degrees) until serving.

Serve with sour cream and applesauce.

Lois Wyse

PINK APPLESAUCE

MAKES 4 CUPS

6–8 large McIntosh apples, quartered,
    cored, and diced (do not peel)
½ cup sugar

½ teaspoon ground cinnamon
    or 2–3 cinnamon sticks
¼ teaspoon nutmeg

In a large pot, mix ingredients together, cover, and cook over low heat until apples are very soft, 20 to 30 minutes. Remove cinnamon sticks, if using. Cool and press mixture through a food mill or sieve to remove peel.

Mashed Potatoes

It's everybody's favorite comfort food, and every grandmother has a favorite way to prepare them. Ritva remembers her Finnish grandmother mashing potatoes with carrots, milk, and chopped raw onion, just for her. Now she does it for her son. Our recipe is simple and traditional.

MAKES 6 TO 8 SERVINGS

4 pounds boiling potatoes, peeled and cut into chunks.
1 tablespoon salt
½ cup butter

½ cup or more milk or half-and-half, warmed
salt and freshly ground black pepper to taste

Put potatoes and salt into a large pot and cover with cold water. Bring to boil. Lower heat, cover, and cook until potatoes are tender, about 25 minutes. Drain. Put potatoes through a ricer or mash by hand, or use an electric mixer. Beat in butter, a little bit at a time. Add milk, salt, and pepper and continue to beat until fluffy but still hot.

Lois Wyse

Scalloped Potatoes

Back in the days when grandmothers worried that the children didn't get enough milk, they plotted and planned ways to put more milk into every dish they could. This was one of them, a family favorite from Nora's Kansas granny.

M A K E S   8   S E R V I N G S

1½ cups half-and-half or milk	3 pounds boiling potatoes, peeled and
1 teaspoon salt	very thinly sliced
¼ teaspoon white pepper	2 tablespoons all-purpose flour
¼ teaspoon paprika	4 tablespoons butter

Preheat oven to 350 degrees. Grease a 9- x 13-inch ovenproof glass baking dish.

Heat half-and-half with salt, pepper, and paprika.

Spread half the potatoes in bottom of baking dish. Sprinkle with 1 tablespoon flour and dot with 2 tablespoons of butter. Repeat with remaining potatoes. Pour in hot half-and-half. Cover with foil and bake 1 hour. Remove foil, and bake until fork-tender and top has browned, about 30 minutes.

Sweet Potato Casserole

Grandmother Frances loved sweet potatoes, but hated gooping them up with marshmallows. She created this casserole, which offers a satisfying alternative for those who need a sweet touch at Thanksgiving.

MAKES 12 TO 14 SERVINGS

3–4 large sweet potatoes, peeled, cut into
    chunks
8 large carrots, peeled, cut into chunks
½ cup fresh orange juice
salt and freshly ground black pepper to
    taste

4 tablespoons unsalted butter
3 tablespoons dark-brown sugar
2 tablespoons dark rum
½ cup pecans, chopped

Preheat oven to 350 degrees. Butter a 2-quart casserole.

Put potatoes, carrots, juice, salt, and pepper together in a large pot and cook until very tender, about 40 minutes.

Mash by hand, or use a food processor or mixer. Beat in butter, brown sugar, and rum. Stir in pecans.

Spoon mixture into casserole and sprinkle with additional chopped pecans and brown sugar, if desired. Bake until top is crisp, about 15 to 20 minutes.

Lois Wyse

Green Beans and Tomatoes

Ahmet remembers his Turkish grandmother's recipe for green beans and tomatoes and, in giving us the recipe, reminds us that this is the kind of food that nurtures memories.

MAKES 8 SERVINGS

2 pounds fresh string beans, trimmed and
    cut in 2-inch pieces
4 tablespoons olive oil
1 large onion, finely chopped
¼ pound smoked ham, shredded
2 large cloves garlic, minced
6 large tomatoes, peeled, seeded, and
    chopped (3 cups well-drained,
    chopped, canned tomatoes may be
    substituted)

1 teaspoon tomato paste, optional
2 tablespoons finely chopped fresh
    parsley
1 tablespoon sugar
salt and freshly
    ground black
    pepper to taste

Cook beans over medium heat in a large pot of boiling water until just tender, 8 to 10 minutes. Do not overcook. Drain and rinse quickly with cold water.

Heat olive oil in a large skillet and sauté onions, ham, and garlic, stirring frequently, until softened, about 5 minutes. Stir in tomatoes, tomato paste, parsley, sugar, salt, and pepper. Bring to a boil.

Lower heat, and cook until mixture thickens and has the consistency of a light sauce. Add string beans to heat through, about 5 minutes. Adjust seasoning, and serve hot or at room temperature.

Stuffed Summer Squash au Gratin

Grandmother used to find squash in her garden long after peas, beans, and carrots had given up their ground. Cinzia, who had a Sicilian grandmother, gave us this recipe. Her grandmother knew that since squash had such a long life, it needed a long list of ways to make it. This is delicious served with marinara sauce (page 159).

MAKES 8 SERVINGS

8 medium zucchini or yellow squash, or a
    combination
2 tablespoons olive oil
2 cloves garlic, minced
¼ cup dried mushrooms, soaked in ¼ cup
    hot water, squeezed and finely
    chopped
½ pound sweet Italian sausage meat,
    finely ground
6 slices prosciutto, finely ground

½ teaspoon rosemary
½ teaspoon basil
2 tablespoons chopped fresh parsley
½ cup fine breadcrumbs
½ cup freshly grated Parmesan cheese
1 egg yolk, lightly beaten
salt and freshly ground black pepper to
    taste
additional grated Parmesan cheese for
    garnish

Bring a large pot of water to boil. Drop in zucchini, and blanch 3 to 5 minutes. Drain, and immediately plunge into cold water. Cut lengthwise, scoop out pulp into a strainer, drain, and reserve. Salt zucchini shells and place on paper towels cut-side down to drain.

Preheat oven to 350 degrees. Lightly oil a 9- or 10-inch baking sheet. Chop the zucchini pulp. Heat oil in skillet and sauté pulp, with garlic, mushrooms, sausage, and ham. Stir, and break up any lumps of sausage meat with wooden spoon. Add the rosemary, basil, and parsley and cook until meat is no longer pink. Mix in breadcrumbs and cheese, and transfer to a bowl. Beat in egg yolk, and let cool slightly. Add the salt and pepper.

Spoon stuffing mixture into zucchini shells, mounding slightly. Sprinkle tops with Parmesan cheese and place on baking sheet. Bake until tops are brown and crisp, about 20 minutes.

Lois Wyse

Eggplant Parmesan

Before many of us knew about pizza, there was eggplant parmesan, a kind of crustless pizza that Candace's St. Louis grandmother often served. Why did Grandmother love to serve this? Because it was yet another way to get reluctant children to eat vegetables.

MAKES 8 SERVINGS

2 large unpeeled eggplants, cut into ½" slices
coarse salt
¼ cup olive oil
½ cup all-purpose flour
2 eggs, lightly beaten with 2 tablespoons
    water

1 cup fine breadcrumbs
3 to 4 cups marinara sauce (recipe
    follows)
1 pound part-skim, low-moisture
    mozzarella cheese, shredded
½ cup grated Parmesan cheese

Preheat oven to 350 degrees. Lay eggplant slices on flat surface. Sprinkle with coarse salt and let stand 30 minutes. (This will give eggplant a smoother flavor and remove bitterness.) Rinse and pat dry with paper towel.

Heat oil in skillet. Dip eggplant slices in flour, eggs, then breadcrumbs. Fry slices over medium heat until golden on each side. Drain on paper towels.

Moisten bottom of 9- x 13-inch ovenproof glass baking dish with 2 or 3 tablespoons of marinara sauce. Add a layer of eggplant slices. Cover with more sauce, mozzarella, and Parmesan. Repeat layers until all ingredients are used. Bake until cheese has melted and browned, about 30 minutes.

MARINARA SAUCE

MAKES 3 TO 4 CUPS

2 tablespoons olive oil
1 small onion, finely chopped
3 garlic cloves, minced
1 1-pound, 14-ounce can tomatoes in
    puree with basil
1 14-ounce can tomato puree

2 tablespoons tomato paste
1 teaspoon chopped dried basil, or 1
    tablespoon fresh
½ teaspoon dried oregano
dash of sugar
salt and freshly ground black pepper to taste

Over medium heat, heat oil in medium saucepan and sauté onion with garlic. Put tomatoes through food mill or processor. Add to pan with the tomato puree, tomato paste, basil, oregano, sugar, salt, and pepper, cover, and simmer 30 minutes.

Chickpeas and Eggplant

A taret was raised in Israel and still makes her grandmother's eggplant. "Food," she explained, "is one way to feel less homesick. I know I'm a grown-up, but when I taste the foods of my childhood, I am never lonely."

MAKES 6 TO 8 SERVINGS

1 large eggplant, peeled and cut into 1-
   inch cubes
1 tablespoon salt
½ cup olive oil
1 large onion, chopped
1 clove garlic
2 cups water
4 large ripe tomatoes, chopped

¼ teaspoon cinnamon
½ teaspoon dried oregano
salt and freshly ground black pepper to
   taste
1 cup canned chickpeas, drained
1 tablespoon freshly squeezed lemon juice
1 teaspoon sugar

Sprinkle eggplant with salt, and leave in a bowl weighted down with a plate, about 30 minutes. Rinse and drain well.

Over medium heat, heat oil in a medium pan and sauté onion and garlic until golden, 2 minutes. Stir in eggplant. Sauté another 2 minutes, stirring well. Add water, tomatoes, cinnamon, and oregano. Add salt and pepper to taste. Cover and simmer 20 minutes.

Add chickpeas and continue cooking until eggplant has softened, about 25 minutes more. Remove from heat and stir in lemon juice and sugar.

May be served hot or cold.

Lois Wyse

D E S S E R T S

NOTHING *TASTES* BETTER THAN THE MEMORY OF SOMETHING A GRANDMOTHER BAKED.

BIG SUGAR COOKIES, FLAKY STRUDELS, chocolate chip cookies made with Grandma's secret ingredients, and pies that cool in the windows of the past, all belong to the generations that follow every grandmother in the kitchen.

Still, not all grandmothers did their big baking at home. Yanne grew up in Norway, and remembers Christmas baking that began many weeks in advance when the village women gathered at the town hall to prepare their goodies. Younger children played in the hall while mothers and grandmothers chopped, peeled, kneaded, cut, and decorated. And sometimes a little wedge of gossip was baked right in the cookies!

Grandmother Nina, who comes to the United States from Greece for Easter every year, arrives with two suitcases, one containing her wardrobe and one full of goodies: pistachios, walnuts, and almonds for toasting; some spices; flour; and almond balls to be dusted with cocoa. She brings moon-shaped cookies, which she powders with confectioners' sugar, cans of honey from her brother's farm, and other sweets and chocolates.

Sometimes we don't have to be grandmothers before we begin to bake like them. I remember a day early in my friendship with Lorraine Smucker when I went to visit her and, after a day of tennis and swimming, we walked into her kitchen where a pie was sitting on the counter. It was the juiciest, best-looking pie I ever saw, and I knew at that minute that even though Lorraine wasn't yet a grandmother, she certainly could bake like one. It's thousands of pies later now, and Lorraine is not only a grandmother but a great-grandmother, and her piecrust recipe (Wait 'til you see the secret!) is here. Of course, the best thing about grandmother desserts is that you're practically begged to take seconds—even if you *don't* eat all your vegetables.

DESSERTS

Baked Apples

Stewed Fruit Compote

Honey Rice Pudding

Bread Pudding with Hard Sauce

Caramel Custard (Flan)

Cherry Clafoutis

Strawberry Shortcake

Fresh Plum Crisp

Blackberry Cobbler

Rhubarb Sheetcake

Pineapple Upside-Down Cake

Angel Food Cake

Chocolate Birthday Cake with Fudge Frosting

Carrot Cake with Cream-Cheese Frosting

Honey Cake

Graham Cracker Cake

Sachertorte

Perfect Pie Crust (9- to 10-inch shell)

Peach Pie Crumble

Apple Pie

Southern Pecan Pie

Lemon Meringue Pie

Mrs. Smucker's Apple Pie

Blueberry Tart

Lemon Squares

Linzer Bars

Mandelbrodt

Rose Wohlgemuth's Poppy Seed-Slices

Rose's Kipfel

Rose's Nut Cups

Apricot Blondies

Almond Shortbread Cookies (Kourambiethes)

Chocolate Toffee Squares

Oatmeal Raisin Crunchies

Baked Apples

No one in the state of Washington ever thought of any dessert that didn't begin with the word *apple*. As Grandma Annie, a native of Washington, used to say, "Anybody who refuses my baked apples cannot possibly have a pure mind." Maybe so but, in addition, if you'd refuse these baked apples, you couldn't have pure taste buds.

MAKES 6 SERVINGS

6 large Rome apples
1 cup white raisins
1 cup chopped walnuts
1 teaspoon cinnamon

12 tablespoons granulated or brown
sugar, or honey
3 teaspoons unsalted butter
Heavy cream for serving, optional

Preheat oven to 375 degrees. Place 1 cup water in a 9- x 9-inch ovenproof glass baking dish. Core the apples. Slice a strip of peel from the top.

Mix together the raisins, walnuts, and cinnamon. Stuff center of each apple with 2 tablespoons of sugar, ½ teaspoon of butter, and some of the raisin and nut mixture. Bake 45 minutes to 1 hour, basting apples twice with water while cooking.

Serve with heavy cream, if desired.

Stewed Fruit Compote

Rhoda's Roumanian grandmother ended every dinner with stewed fruit compote. She believed it was good for the digestion, and Rhoda said, "I don't remember ever getting sick after eating at Grandma's. It was those hamburgers and colas and fries followed by chocolate sundaes with whipped cream that did me in."

MAKES 8 SERVINGS

4 cups mixed dried fruits, such as
    apricots, peaches, apples, pears, or
    cherries
1 cup pitted prunes
½ cup white raisins
1 cup white wine or water
1 orange, rind grated, and juiced

¼ teaspoon grated nutmeg
¼ teaspoon allspice
¼ cup dark-brown sugar
2–3 cinnamon sticks
toasted sliced almonds for garnish,
    optional
Sour cream for garnish, optional

Combine dried fruits, prunes, raisins, and wine and soak for several hours or overnight to plump. Put fruit and wine in pot and mix in rind, juice, nutmeg, allspice, sugar, and cinnamon sticks. Cover, and simmer 30 minutes or until fruit is tender. Remove cinnamon sticks.

May be served hot or at room temperature sprinkled with almonds and a dollop of sour cream.

Honey Rice Pudding

When we asked both men and women to name their favorite comfort foods, rice pudding was high on every list. Perhaps that is because rice is the first grain most of us ever taste and, so, rice pudding takes us back in our heads and hearts to our own childhood. One reason that we used this particular recipe is that a grandmother can play a game with her grandchildren when she adds an almond to the recipe, and promises that whoever finds that single hidden almond will also find that wishes do come true.

MAKES 6 TO 8 SERVINGS

1 cup long-grain rice	3 eggs, lightly beaten
3 cups whole milk	1 whole natural almond
1 cup heavy cream	½ teaspoon cinnamon
½ teaspoon salt	¼ teaspoon nutmeg
1 teaspoon vanilla extract	Heavy cream or whipped cream for
½ cup sugar	garnish, optional
¼ cup honey	

Preheat oven to 350 degrees. Butter a 2-quart casserole.

Put rice in a saucepan, cover with cold water, bring to a boil, and cook 10 minutes. Drain and rinse with cold water.

In a bowl, combine milk, cream, salt, vanilla, sugar, and honey. Stir in rice, eggs, almond, cinnamon, and nutmeg. Pour into prepared casserole and bake one hour, or until rice is tender and pudding is thick and creamy.

Serve warm or cold. May be served with heavy cream or a dollop of whipped cream.

Lois Wyse

Bread Pudding with Hard Sauce

Constance recalled that her English grandmother never wasted a crumb of her own home-baked bread. She sliced it (for sandwiches); she diced it (for croutons in her homemade soup); and then, just before she turned it into breadcrumbs, she made bread pudding. This is her old Midlands recipe.

MAKES 6 SERVINGS

*1 loaf stale French bread or egg bread
   (such as challah)*

2 cups milk

3 eggs, beaten

1 teaspoon vanilla

1 tablespoon cinnamon

½ cup light brown sugar

1 cup raisins

½ cup chopped nuts (walnuts or pecans)

*1 Granny Smith apple, peeled and
   chopped*

8 tablespoons unsalted butter, melted

¼ teaspoon salt

Hard sauce (recipe follows)

Preheat oven to 350 degrees. Butter 6 12-ounce ramekins, or a 1½ quart baking dish.

Break bread into small pieces into a bowl, add milk, and leave to soak for 20 minutes.

Mash bread with the eggs, vanilla, cinnamon, and sugar. Fold in raisins, chopped nuts, apples, butter, and salt.

Pour into ramekins and bake 15 to 20 minutes or 40 to 50 minutes in a baking dish until browned and set in the middle. Serve with hard sauce.

HARD SAUCE

¼ cup unsalted butter

1 cup confectioners' sugar

½ cup brandy

¼ teaspoon cinnamon

Beat butter with sugar until creamy. Beat in brandy and cinnamon. Serve over hot pudding.

Caramel Custard
(Flan)

The baked egg custard is a worldwide spoon-food dessert. There is a Chinese baked custard dessert, and certainly every cuisine in Europe has its version. The one we've selected is from Grandmother Manuela, who comes from northern Spain. You'll find this recipe travels well.

MAKES 4 TO 6 SERVINGS

1 cup sugar	3 eggs
2½ cups milk	3 egg yolks
1 teaspoon vanilla extract (or 1 vanilla bean)	

Preheat oven to 350 degrees. Have ready a one-quart ring mold or soufflé dish.

Heat ½ cup sugar in a small heavy saucepan. As sugar melts, rotate pan and continue to cook until caramelized, about 10 minutes. Quickly pour caramel into the mold, tilting dish back and forth, to coat bottom evenly. Leave to cool.

Bring milk with vanilla (or vanilla bean) slowly to a boil and remove from heat (discard bean). Beat eggs, egg yolks, and remaining sugar together to combine well. Gradually whisk in milk in a steady stream, beating constantly.

Pour mixture into mold, place it into a large baking pan of hot water reaching two-thirds of the way up the sides.

Bake flan 1 hour, or until a knife comes out clean from the center. Remove from water bath, cool, and chill flan at least 6 hours.

To unmold, dip bottom of mold in hot water briefly to loosen, and run a metal spatula around edge of dish. Invert onto serving plate by placing serving dish upside down on top and reversing dishes quickly. Spoon caramel over each serving.

Lois Wyse

Cherry Clafoutis

ountry French furniture and country French cooking all are a part of our lives. That means that somewhere, someone in her country French house must try this most French of country desserts given to us by Marie Josette, a grandmother from Provence.

MAKES 8 SERVINGS

2 cups pitted black Bing cherries, well-drained

4 eggs

2 egg yolks

½ cup sugar

1 cup all-purpose flour

1 tablespoon unsalted butter, melted

2¼ cups milk

2 tablespoons kirsch (cherry brandy)

1 teaspoon vanilla extract

dash salt

confectioners' sugar, for garnish

Preheat oven to 350 degrees. Butter a shallow 6-cup glass dish.

Scatter cherries over the bottom. In a blender or food processor, combine the eggs, yolks, sugar, flour, butter, milk, kirsch, vanilla, and salt. Process until smooth. Pour the custard mixture over the cherries. Dot with a little butter and sprinkle of sugar.

Bake one hour, or until the top is puffy and golden. Serve at room temperature, garnished with a sprinkle of confectioners' sugar.

Strawberry Shortcake

Raise the flag, bring out the charcoal—we're about to celebrate Memorial Day, Fourth of July, and any summer birthday or holiday you have in mind. And for dessert, we'll take Grandmother Bess' strawberry shortcake—it's a winner from Southern California.

MAKES 6 SERVINGS

2 cups all-purpose flour
2 tablespoons sugar
3 teaspoons baking powder
½ teaspoon salt
4 tablespoons unsalted butter

1 large egg, beaten
⅔ cup heavy cream
4 cups of sweet strawberries (or other summer berries)
1 cup heavy cream, whipped

Preheat oven to 450 degrees.

Sift flour with other dry ingredients. Cut butter into flour until mixture resembles coarse crumbs. Combine egg with cream and stir into flour to moisten.

Turn dough out onto a floured surface, knead gently for 30 seconds, and roll out to ½-inch thick. Using a 3½-inch or 4-inch cookie cutter (round or fluted), cut out 6 rounds. Bake 10 minutes on an ungreased cookie sheet.

TO SERVE

Have ready 6 dessert plates. Split a shortcake in half, top with some berries, a dollop of whipped cream, and the other half of the shortcake.

Serve while shortcakes are still warm.

Lois Wyse

Fresh Plum Crisp

There are crisps and crumbles and brown betties. Where your granny grew up determines the recipes handed down in your family. The recipe we like for this crisp is Polish and comes from a friend who is Russian, Polish, and Slav, which means she had a variety of grandmother recipes handed down. By the way, the best time to make this is at the end of summer when the oval prune plums are in season.

MAKES 8 TO 10 SERVINGS

1¾ cups all-purpose flour

12 tablespoons unsalted butter

1½ cups sugar

1 teaspoon vanilla extract

1 large egg

1 teaspoon baking powder

dash salt

2 pounds ripe, dark plums, pitted

2 tablespoons plum brandy or rum

dash cinnamon

dash nutmeg

dash ground cloves

¼ cup chopped walnuts

vanilla ice cream or whipped cream for serving, optional

Preheat oven to 350 degrees.

Place 1 cup flour, 4 tablespoons butter, ½ cup sugar, vanilla, egg, baking powder, and salt into mixing bowl and mix well until smooth. Press firmly over bottom of 9- x 13-inch glass ovenproof baking dish, working some of the dough up the sides about ¼ inch. Set aside.

Melt 4 tablespoons butter in skillet, and stir in ¼ cup sugar. Allow sugar to melt, add plums, and cook five minutes. Add brandy or rum and spices, cook a few minutes more. Spread over prepared dough.

Using fingertips, rub remaining flour, butter, and sugar together. Add walnuts, and a dash each of cinnamon and nutmeg. Sprinkle evenly over plums. Dot with butter and bake 45 minutes, or until top is brown and crisp.

Serve warm with vanilla ice cream or whipped cream.

Blackberry Cobbler

When Grandmother went out into the berry patch, it was not just for the fresh air and sunshine. Grandmother was looking for berries to make her cobbler. The recipe we like comes from Ingrid, who learned it from her Michigan grandmother, and her blackberry cobbler will keep everybody coming back for more. This same recipe is just as good with raspberries or blueberries, or a combination.

MAKES 4 TO 6 SERVINGS

8 tablespoons unsalted butter, at room temperature

½ cup plus ⅓ cup sugar

1 egg yolk

¼ teaspoon vanilla

½ cup all-purpose flour

¼ teaspoon baking powder

⅛ teaspoon salt

4 cups blackberries

1 tablespoon cornstarch

1 teaspoon vanilla extract

ice cream, optional

Preheat oven to 375 degrees. Butter a 4-cup shallow glass baking dish or 8-inch-square glass pan. Beat butter and ½ cup sugar together until blended. Beat in egg and vanilla. Sift flour with baking powder and salt, and stir until combined.

Toss berries with cornstarch, ⅓ cup sugar, and vanilla extract. Pour prepared berries into baking dish. Drop spoonfuls of dough on top of berries. Sprinkle lightly with additional sugar.

Bake 45 minutes or until pastry is golden. Serve with ice cream, if desired.

Lois Wyse

Rhubarb Sheetcake

If you had a rhubarb patch in your backyard (that's what grandmothers called lawns), then your grandmother probably had a recipe for a rhubarb cake. This one is from Gwyneth, an English grandmother, but it could just as easily have come from a Midwestern grandmother, because the rhubarb grows thick and good in both places.

MAKES 12 SERVINGS

¾ cup unsalted butter (1½ sticks)
2 cups dark-brown sugar (firmly packed)
2 large eggs
3 cups sifted all-purpose flour
¾ teaspoon salt
1½ teaspoons baking soda
1½ cups milk
1½ teaspoons vanilla extract
3 cups rhubarb, cut into ¾-inch pieces, or
    use 1 1-pound bag, frozen

1 Bosc pear or apple, chopped
grated rind of 1 lemon
1 tablespoon sugar
1 teaspoon cinnamon
1 tablespoon fresh lemon juice
confectioners' sugar, for serving
vanilla ice cream, optional, for
    serving

Preheat oven to 350 degrees. Grease and flour a 9- x 13-inch baking pan.

Cream butter with sugar. Beat eggs into butter mixture. Sift flour again with salt and baking soda. Add flour to butter mixture, alternating with milk, beating well after each addition. Stir in vanilla, rhubarb, pear or apple, and lemon rind. Spread batter in prepared pan. Mix sugar and cinnamon. Sprinkle with sugar and cinnamon and lemon juice.

Bake on middle rack for 1 hour, or until toothpick comes clean when inserted into middle of cake.

Dust with confectioners' sugar just before serving. Delicious with a scoop of vanilla ice cream.

Pineapple Upside-Down Cake

From the beginning of time grandmothers have been showing their touch of Houdini to grandchildren by promising them an upside-down cake, a dessert that has such a childish ring that—even if the cake weren't as good as it is—children would eat it with delight. Our cake came to us from Rosamunde, who spent part of every childhood summer with her grandmother in Maryland.

MAKES 8 SERVINGS

4 tablespoons unsalted butter	½ cup maraschino cherries
1 cup dark brown sugar	½ cup pecans
8 slices canned pineapple, drained	

BATTER

4 eggs	1 teaspoon lemon zest
1 cup sugar	½ teaspoon vanilla
1 cup flour	Ice cream or whipped cream, optional, for
1 heaping teaspoon baking powder	serving

Preheat oven to 325 degrees.

Melt butter in the bottom of 9-inch round baking pan, and stir in brown sugar. Place pineapple slices flat in pan and decorate with cherries and pecans.

PREPARE BATTER:

Beat eggs with sugar until thick and creamy, about 10 minutes. Sift flour with baking powder. Beat sifted flour, lemon zest, and vanilla into egg mixture. Pour batter over pineapple, and bake 45 minutes to one hour.

Run sharp knife around side of pan and immediately invert cake onto serving plate. Leave pan on top of cake 10 minutes, then carefully remove. Serve warm with whipped cream or topped with ice cream.

Lois Wyse

Angel Food Cake

Grandmothers were baking this fat-free cake (no butter or egg yolks here) even before they knew that fats aren't good for us and that eggs might not be the most healthful food. And grandmothers even knew how long to bake the cake with no calibrated ovens and no push buttons, so that the cake never fell from the tube pan before its time. Angel food cake was one of my mother's specialties because my father was on a restricted diet, and every time I see an angel food cake, I remember my own family dinners.

MAKES 10 TO 12 SERVINGS

1 cup sifted all-purpose flour
1¼ cups sifted confectioners' sugar
1½ cups egg whites (12 large eggs)
1½ teaspoons cream of tartar

¼ teaspoon salt
1½ teaspoons vanilla extract
¼ teaspoon almond extract
1 cup sugar

Preheat oven to 375 degrees.

Sift flour with confectioners' sugar three times. Beat egg whites with cream of tartar, salt, and vanilla and almond extracts until stiff enough to hold soft peaks. Beat in granulated sugar, 2 tablespoons at a time, and continue beating until meringue holds stiff peaks. Sift ¼ of the flour mixture over egg whites and fold in gently. Continue this process until all of flour has been added. Gently spoon batter into ungreased 10-inch tube pan.

Bake until top is golden brown and springs back lightly to the touch, about 30 minutes. Invert onto rack and allow cake to cool completely before removing the pan.

VARIATION FOR CHOCOLATE LOVERS:

Sift ⅓ cup Dutch-process cocoa powder with flour and confectioners' sugar; ⅓ cup mini chocolate chips can also be folded into finished batter just before baking. Serve with cocoa-flavored sweetened whipped cream.

Chocolate Birthday Cake with Fudge Frosting

What child doesn't love his birthday? And what child doesn't love his birthday even more when it's celebrated with a chocolate birthday cake? This is an old-fashioned family recipe from a Texas grandmother who has twelve grandchildren—so she bakes this cake twelve times a year. Her eldest grandchild is now 22, and he still comes home for some of that Grandma Birthday Cake.

MAKES 10 TO 12 SERVINGS

10 tablespoons unsalted butter, at room temperature

1¾ cups sugar

2 large eggs

1 teaspoon vanilla

2½ cups all-purpose flour

1¼ teaspoons baking soda

½ teaspoon salt

2½ ounces unsweetened chocolate, melted and cooled

1¼ cups ice water

fudge frosting (recipe follows)

Preheat oven to 350 degrees. Butter 2 9-inch cake pans, line with waxed paper, and butter again.

Cream butter, sugar, eggs, and vanilla until light and creamy, and continue beating about 5 minutes on high speed. Sift flour with baking soda and salt. Blend in melted chocolate, add sifted flour alternating with ice water, starting and ending with dry ingredients. Mix well after each addition.

Lois Wyse

Pour batter into pans, and bake 30 minutes or until sides shrink slightly and cake springs back when touched lightly. Allow to cool 2 minutes before inverting onto cake racks. Carefully remove wax paper and prepare icing.

FUDGE FROSTING

3 1-ounce squares unsweetened chocolate
3 tablespoons unsalted butter, softened
2 cups confectioners' sugar

⅓ cup milk or cream
1 teaspoon vanilla
dash of salt

Melt chocolate and butter in top of double boiler. Cool slightly. Stir in sugar, milk, vanilla, and salt, and transfer to bowl of an electric mixer. Beat until thick and spreadable. If too thick, thin with a teaspoon of milk—if too thin, add more confectioners' sugar. Frost between layers and sides and top of cake.

Carrot Cake with Cream-Cheese Frosting

Nobody's grandmother brought this cake from Paris or Moscow or Athens; it is as American as the baked potato. The first grandmothers we know who made this are from Philadelphia, which is appropriate since Philadelphia was one of the first American cities and cream cheese is native to America.

MAKES 8 TO 10 SERVINGS

1 cup vegetable oil

2 cups sugar

4 large eggs, lightly beaten

2 cups all-purpose flour

1 teaspoon ground cinnamon

½ teaspoon nutmeg

2 teaspoons baking powder

1½ teaspoons baking soda

1 teaspoon salt

2 cups grated carrots

1 cup crushed pineapple, drained well

1 cup chopped walnuts

cream-cheese frosting (recipe follows)

Preheat oven to 350 degrees. Grease a 9- x 13-inch baking pan.

Beat oil, sugar, and eggs together until thick. Stir flour with dry ingredients and add to egg mixture. Stir in carrots, pineapple, and walnuts. Pour into baking pan, and bake 45 minutes. Allow cake to cool 10 minutes before inverting onto cake rack. Cool completely before icing.

CREAM-CHEESE FROSTING

8 ounces cream cheese

6 ounces unsalted butter

2 cups confectioners' sugar

1 teaspoon vanilla extract

1 teaspoon grated orange rind

Beat all ingredients together until smooth. Frost cake and cut into squares.

Lois Wyse

Honey Cake

Sherri reminds us that in Jewish households this is a traditional dessert for Chanukah, and is also a traditional dessert to celebrate a baby-naming, because honey is supposed to represent the sweetness of life.

5 eggs
1½ cups sugar
¾ cup vegetable oil
1½ cups honey
3½ cups all-purpose flour
4 teaspoons baking powder
1 teaspoon baking soda
½ teaspoon salt

½ teaspoon ground cloves
½ teaspoon allspice
1 cup cold strong coffee
1½ teaspoons anise seed (or extract)
1 cup chopped walnuts (mixed with ¼ cup flour)
confectioners' sugar, for serving

Preheat oven to 350 degrees. Grease a 9- x 13-inch baking pan, line bottom with wax paper, and grease again.

Beat eggs in large bowl until light. Add sugar gradually and continue to beat until light and fluffy. Add oil and honey and beat well. Sift flour twice with dry ingredients.

Add flour to egg mixture, alternating with coffee, starting and ending with flour. Add anise and chopped nuts and pour batter into pan. Bake until golden, 1 hour.

Cool 10 minutes before inverting onto cake rack. Carefully remove wax paper. Turn right-side up and allow to cool.

This cake is even more delicious when it is made a day in advance. Sprinkle with confectioners' sugar just before serving.

Graham Cracker Cake

Kathy Hagstrom would probably have been more willing to part with her paycheck than this recipe. It was a recipe used by her mother and grandmother; no one ever gave her the precise directions, but she reproduced the taste after years of experimenting. So thank you, Kathy—lots of grandchildren are going to be thrilled that there is yet another way to love graham crackers.

MAKES 8 TO 10 SERVINGS

8 tablespoons unsalted butter

1 cup sugar

3 eggs, separated

1 teaspoon vanilla

½ cup all-purpose flour

½ teaspoon salt

2 teaspoons baking powder

1 cup milk

½ pound honey graham crackers, finely ground

2 cups heavy cream, whipped, for serving

1 pint fresh strawberries, sliced, for serving

Preheat oven to 350 degrees. Butter and flour two 9-inch round cake pans.

Cream butter and sugar until fluffy. Add egg yolks, one at a time, and beat until mixture is creamy. Add vanilla.

Sift flour with salt and baking powder. Stir in sifted flour, alternating with milk, one-third at a time. Fold in graham cracker crumbs. Whip egg whites until firm peaks form and fold into cake batter.

Pour into pans and bake until cake springs back lightly to the touch, 20 to 25 minutes.

Cool 5 minutes before turning out onto cake rack to cool completely.

TO SERVE:

Spread top of one layer with whipped cream, place second cake on top, cover with remaining whipped cream and sliced fruit.

This cake can also be made in a 9- x 12-inch baking pan, dusted with confectioners' sugar, cut into squares, and served plain.

Lois Wyse

Sachertorte

As most of us know, the Sachertorte was first served (and still is) at the Hotel Sacher in Vienna. Austrian grandmothers never claim to have the original hotel recipe; instead they lay claim to their unique interpretations. This one is from Grobmutter Gretchen.

MAKES 8 TO 10 SERVINGS

3 1-ounce squares unsweetened chocolate	2 eggs
1⅔ cup sugar, divided	2 cups all-purpose flour
1 cup milk, divided	1 teaspoon baking soda
1 egg, lightly beaten	¼ teaspoon salt
8 tablespoons unsalted butter	1 jar apricot preserves, heated and sieved
1 cup sugar	to remove lumps
1 teaspoon vanilla	1 cup whipped cream

Preheat oven to 350 degrees. Butter two 9-inch cake pans lined with waxed paper.

Combine chocolate, ⅔ cup sugar, ½ cup milk, and lightly beaten egg in small saucepan. Stir over low heat until smooth and thick. *Do not boil.* Transfer to a bowl to cool.

Beat butter, 1 cup sugar, and vanilla until light and fluffy. Beat in 2 eggs one at a time.

Sift flour with baking soda and salt. Add flour mixture one-third at a time, alternating with remaining milk. Stir in cooled chocolate. Pour batter into baking pans. Bake until cake springs back when touched lightly, 20 to 25 minutes.

Cool 5 minutes before inverting cake onto rack. Cool completely. Split cakes in half to create 4 layers. Put one layer on rack over tray, spread with apricot preserves and chocolate icing (recipe follows). Cover remaining layers similarly, taking care to save enough icing for top and sides of cake. Allow any excess icing to drip down onto tray below. Icing will become hard and shiny after several hours of refrigeration. Thinly slice, topping each serving with whipped cream (known in Austria as *mit schlag*).

TIP: *To split the cakes evenly take a long piece of thread and hold it taut. Using a gentle sawing motion, pull it through the cake horizontally.*

continued on next page

CHOCOLATE GLAZE ICING

8 1-ounce squares unsweetened chocolate

8 tablespoons unsalted butter

2 cups confectioners' sugar

dash salt

2 teaspoons vanilla extract

Melt chocolate with butter in top of double boiler. Stir until smooth. Transfer to bowl and combine with confectioners' sugar, salt, and vanilla. Add about 2 tablespoons boiling water 1 tablespoon at a time until icing is smooth and shiny.

Lois Wyse

Perfect Pie Crust

(9- to 10-inch shell)

Grandmother knew that the secret of a pie was a mighty good crust. We have reviewed hundreds of grandmother piecrusts, and grandmothers Sherri and Liza selected this as our choice for a never-fail crust that works with almost any kind of filling. We've included three of our (and our children's, and grandchildren's) favorites.

1½ cups flour, preferably bleached flour
    or pastry flour
½ teaspoon salt
2 teaspoons sugar
4 tablespoons cold unsalted butter, cut
    into bits

4 tablespoons vegetable
    shortening
1 teaspoon freshly grated
    lemon rind
3–4 tablespoons ice
    water

Preheat oven to 400 degrees. Put all the ingredients except the ice water into a bowl of an electric mixer and set at low speed. Mix until flour mixture resembles fine grains of sand. Begin adding ice water, one tablespoon at a time, until dough forms a ball.

Remove the dough, wrap in wax paper, and refrigerate 30 minutes.

On lightly floured surface, with floured rolling pin, roll dough out into a circle to fit pie plate. Try to work gently and quickly. Transfer dough to 9- to 10-inch pie plate. Trim off any excess. Crimp edges.

Cover top of dough with wax paper. Fill bottom with dried beans, raw rice, or aluminum nuggets. Partially bake crust 10 minutes. Remove wax paper and beans carefully. For fully baked shell, return to oven for another 7 to 8 minutes until golden. For a pie with a top crust, double the recipe. The bottom crust will require more dough than the top crust.

TIP: *Glass pie pan produces a crisper, golden crust, desirable for fruit pies. Put pie on a baking sheet to pick up any overflow during baking. It will also be helpful when moving the pie in and out of the oven.*

Peach Pie Crumble

5 cups ripe, peeled, and sliced peaches
   (about 8 medium), preferably
   freestone
¼ cup dark-brown sugar
¼ cup sugar
3 tablespoons cornstarch

¼ teaspoon nutmeg
¼ teaspoon cinnamon
pinch of salt
1 tablespoon lemon juice
1 9- to 10-inch pie shell, partially baked
   (see p. 183)

CRUMBLE TOPPING

2 tablespoons unsalted butter
1 cup sugar
½ cup all-purpose flour
1 teaspoon baking powder

½ teaspoon salt
½ teaspoon ground ginger
¾ cup sliced almonds, crushed
½ cup rolled oats (oatmeal)

vanilla ice cream, for serving

Toss peaches with sugars. Allow to stand one hour. Drain and reserve juices.

Preheat oven to 400 degrees.

Combine peach juice, cornstarch, spices, and salt in a small saucepan. Cook over low heat until thick and clear, stirring constantly. Combine with drained peaches, add lemon juice, and spoon mixture into the partially baked pie shell.

PREPARE CRUMBLE TOPPING:

Using fingertips, mix all the ingredients together. Sprinkle over prepared pie shell. Put into preheated oven 10 minutes. Reduce heat to 350 degrees, and continue baking for another 45 minutes. Serve with vanilla ice cream.

TIP: *To peel peaches, immerse in boiling water for 30 seconds. Plunge into cold water and peel.*

Lois Wyse

Apple Pie

*1 double recipe for 9- to 10-inch unbaked
 pie shell (see p. 183)*
*8–10 large tart apples (about 5 pounds),
 peeled, cored, cut into thick slices*
1½ cups sugar

¼ cup all-purpose flour
1½ teaspoons cinnamon
¼ teaspoon nutmeg
dash salt
2 tablespoons unsalted butter

Preheat oven to 400 degrees.

In a large bowl, thoroughly combine apples, sugar, flour, cinnamon, nutmeg, and salt.

Roll out pastry into a 16- to 18-inch circle. Carefully slide into 9- or 10-inch pie plate, allowing pastry to hang over sides. Pile apple mixture up high, and dot with butter. Fold pastry up over apples, leaving an opening at the top.

Bake until golden, 50 minutes.

Southern Pecan Pie

1 9- to 10-inch partially baked pie shell
   (see page 183)
⅔ cup sugar
3 eggs
1 cup dark corn syrup

dash salt
5 tablespoons unsalted butter, melted
2 cups pecan halves
whipped cream for garnish, optional

Preheat oven to 350 degrees.

    Beat together sugar, eggs, corn syrup, and salt. Stir in butter. Pour into pie shell and top with pecans.

    Bake until knife comes out clean when inserted into center, about 50 minutes. Serve warm, with dollop of whipped cream.

Lemon Meringue Pie

MAKES 8 SERVINGS

1 9- to 10-inch pie shell, fully baked
   (see page 183)

FILLING

½ cup cornstarch

1½ cups water

1½ cups sugar

4 egg yolks, lightly beaten

½ cup fresh lemon juice

grated rind of 1 lemon

Pinch salt

2 tablespoons unsalted butter

MERINGUE TOPPING

4 egg whites

¼ teaspoon cream of tartar

6 tablespoons superfine sugar

PREPARE FILLING:

In a pot over low heat, stir cornstarch with water until dissolved. Add sugar, whisking well, bring to a boil, and remove from heat. Stir 2 tablespoons of hot liquid into egg yolks to warm them. Add eggs to remaining cornstarch mixture. Stir in the lemon juice, rind, and salt, and mix well.

Cook mixture over very low heat stirring constantly, until thickened, about 2 minutes. *Do not boil.* Stir in butter. Cover tightly with plastic wrap, and chill thoroughly. Spoon into prepared pie shell.

PREPARE MERINGUE:

Preheat broiler, and adjust rack. Whip egg whites with cream of tartar until soft peaks form. Gradually add sugar and continue to beat until stiff and shiny. Use rubber spatula to scoop meringue onto top of lemon filling, forming soft peaks. Slide under broiler for a minute until meringue browns. Watch carefully; the meringue must not burn. Serve at once.

Mrs. Smucker's Apple Pie

Here is my friend Lorraine Smucker's apple pie. Everyone knows that with a name like Smucker's it has to be good, but if it's a Lorraine Smucker apple pie, it's not just good—it's the best. The secret that makes this pie different from the others is a *hot*-water crust!

APPLE FILLING

5–6 large Granny Smith apples, peeled, cored, and sliced	1 cup sugar 2 teaspoons ground cinnamon

CRUST

1 cup vegetable shortening 1 teaspoon salt ⅓ cup boiling water	2⅓ cups all-purpose flour 2 tablespoons unsalted butter 2 tablespoons milk or cream

Preheat oven to 400 degrees.

Mix the apples, sugar, and cinnamon together and set aside.

In large mixing bowl, combine shortening, salt, and water. Mix well with a fork until fluffy. Add flour all at once, and continue to mix until mixture forms a soft ball of dough. Divide in half.

Dust rolling pin well with flour and roll one-half of dough on well-floured pastry cloth to fit 9-inch deep-dish pie plate. Spoon in filling and dot with butter. Roll out remaining dough, place over filling, and flute edges of top and bottom crust together. Cut several slits in top crust and brush with milk.

Bake in center of oven for 15 minutes, reduce heat to 375 degrees, and continue baking an additional 45 minutes.

NOTE: *This makes an absolutely delicious crust; however, it is very sticky and delicate to work with. Do not be alarmed. Continue to flour your rolling pin and pinch any holes together as you work. We used a 9-inch deep-dish glass pie plate. Flip dough over rolling pin to transfer from board to pie plate. Your crust may be uneven but it will have a wonderful rustic look after baking.*

Blueberry Tart

Great-grandmother Violet lived in Finland and had a summer house on a Baltic island; her children, grandchildren, and great-grandchildren looked forward to visiting her each summer. The grandchildren knew that their job was to go out into the woods each day and pick the blueberries for that day's tart. Nina, the cook, would wait for the baskets to come to the kitchen and begin to bake until dinner time. The great-grandchildren still remember their summer badge: blue teeth from eating everything Nina baked.

MAKES 12 SERVINGS

1 egg

½ cup heavy cream

8 tablespoons unsalted butter

2½ cups all-purpose flour

FILLING

6 cups fresh blueberries

½ cup sugar, or enough to cover the
    berries

½ cup crushed sugar cookies

Preheat oven to 375 degrees.

Mix the egg, cream, butter, and flour together in food processor. Dough will be sticky. Wrap in waxed paper and chill ½ hour.

Roll out dough on floured surface. Line 12- x 18- x 1-inch cookie sheet with dough, reaching halfway up sides. Spread with berries, sprinkle with sugar and cookie crumbs. Bake about 20 minutes.

Lemon Squares

There isn't a church or village cookbook that doesn't contain a recipe for lemon squares. Everybody likes the way lemon flavor skips over the taste buds after a meal. This recipe was made by a friend of ours, a grandmother in Atlanta.

MAKES ABOUT 16 SQUARES

12 tablespoons unsalted butter (¾ cup)	2 eggs, beaten
¼ cup confectioners' sugar	1 cup sugar
1 cup all-purpose flour, plus 2 tablespoons	3 tablespoons lemon juice
	grated rind of 1 lemon

Preheat oven to 350 degrees.

Blend butter with confectioners' sugar and beat in 1 cup of flour. Pat dough into bottom of 8-inch-square baking pan. Bake for 15 minutes until golden.

Beat eggs with sugar. Combine reserved flour with lemon juice and grated rind, and add to egg mixture. Blend well and pour over crust.

Bake 15 minutes until firm. Use a sieve to dust with confectioners' sugar. Cut around edges of pan while square is still hot, but allow to cool before cutting into serving squares.

Lois Wyse

Linzer Bars

From the coffee houses of Europe to the coffee bars of the United States, linzer bars are a favorite accompaniment. Some flavors just marry well with coffee, and who knew that better than a grandmother? This recipe is from a Munich grossmutter.

MAKES 36 BARS

8 tablespoons unsalted butter
½ cup light brown sugar
½ cup white sugar
1 cup blanched almonds, toasted and
    finely chopped
1 egg, lightly beaten
1½ cups all-purpose flour

1 teaspoon baking powder
1 teaspoon cinnamon
¼ teaspoon ground cloves
1 tablespoon cocoa
1 cup raspberry jam
grated rind of 1 lemon
confectioners' sugar, for serving

Preheat oven to 375 degrees.

Cream butter with sugars until light and fluffy. Beat in the nuts and egg. Sift flour with baking powder, cinnamon, cloves, and cocoa. Mix into butter mixture to form a dough. Press two-thirds of dough into 9- x 13-inch baking pan. Mix raspberry jam and lemon rind, and spread over dough.

Roll out the remaining dough between two pieces of wax paper to ¼-inch thickness. Refrigerate 30 minutes. Cut into ½-inch strips, and place over jam to create a lattice top.

Bake 30 minutes. Allow to cool completely before cutting into 1½-inch squares. Sprinkle with confectioners' sugar before serving.

Mandelbrodt

Our friend Marlene remembers getting care packages from *Bubbie*, her grandmother, all the years she was in college. Included, of course, was mandelbrodt because it is the one dessert that never arrived stale (if it did, who could tell? Mandelbrodt is crisper than biscotti). When her grandmother died, Marlene kept the one piece of mandelbrodt that she had left from the last package. She put it in the freezer, thought about having it bronzed, but finally decided to let mandelbrodt live in her memory.

MAKES 5 DOZEN

½ cup sugar
½ cup vegetable oil plus 3 tablespoons, divided
2 eggs, beaten
1 teaspoon vanilla extract
¾ cup golden raisins
¾ cup whole almonds, finely ground
2¼ cups flour
1 teaspoon baking powder
⅛ teaspoon baking soda
¼ cup sugar
1 tablespoon cinnamon

Preheat oven to 350 degrees. Coat a cookie sheet with 3 tablespoons of oil.

In a large bowl, cream sugar and ½ cup oil. Mix in eggs and vanilla, and beat well. Stir in raisins and ground almonds.

Sift flour with baking powder and baking soda. Gradually add sifted flour to mixture, and combine well. Knead together until smooth and slightly firm.

Divide dough into four balls. Form each ball into a 16- to 18-inch log. Place logs on cookie sheet and roll in oil. Mix sugar and cinnamon and sprinkle over logs.

Bake 20 minutes. Cool slightly, about 10 minutes. Using tip of sharp knife, cut each roll into 1-inch diagonal slices. Return pieces to cookie sheet, and bake 20 minutes more or until golden.

Lois Wyse

Rose Wohlgemuth's Poppy-Seed Slices

My childhood is coated in poppy seed, because my mother made the best poppy-seed dessert in all the world. Wherever she went, those poppy-seed rolls went, too. She also made a nut version called *kipfel*. These recipes, on little recipe index cards, are now in kitchens from California to New York. Grandmas may not travel a lot, but their recipes certainly do.

MAKES ABOUT 50 PIECES

16 tablespoons unsalted butter, plus 2
    tablespoons, for spreading
2 cups all-purpose flour
2 cups sour cream
1 tablespoon sugar

1 teaspoon vanilla
2 12½-ounce cans Solo Poppy seed
    filling, at room temperature
¼ cup milk
¼ cup confectioners' sugar, for serving

Mix butter, flour, sour cream, sugar, and vanilla together to form a smooth dough. Divide into three balls, and chill several hours or overnight.

Preheat oven to 350 degrees. Roll out each ball on floured surface to form a 10- x 16-inch rectangle. Trim away uneven ends.

Brush with melted butter and spread 1 cup poppy-seed filling over each rectangle, leaving a 1-inch border all around. Roll up dough the long way, jelly-roll style, and place on 18-inch cookie sheet. Roll should be approximately 3 inches wide x 16 inches long. Brush lightly with milk and sprinkle top with sugar, if desired.

Bake in middle of oven until golden brown, about 30 minutes. Allow to cool.

Cut roll into ¾- to 1-inch slices and dust lightly with confectioners' sugar.

Rose's Kipfel

2 cups all-purpose flour
16 tablespoons unsalted butter
1 cup sour cream

1 tablespoon sugar
¼ teaspoon vanilla
½ teaspoon salt

FILLING

¼ cup chopped raisins, optional
½ cup mixed chopped nuts, such as
    walnuts, pecans, or almonds, finely
    chopped

½ cup sugar
1 teaspoon ground cinnamon
grated rind of 1 lemon

Mix flour, butter, sour cream, sugar, vanilla, and salt together to form a soft dough. Form into 3 balls and refrigerate overnight.

Preheat oven to 350 degrees.

Mix raisins, nuts, sugar, cinnamon, and lemon rind together in a small bowl.

Roll out each ball of dough onto floured surface to form three 12-inch circles. With a sharp knife, cut each circle into 12 pie-shaped wedges. Drop a teaspoon of nut mixture at the wider end of each wedge. Roll up toward the center.

Transfer to cookie sheets. Brush with milk and sprinkle with any remaining nut-cinnamon mixture. Bake 10 to 15 minutes or until golden.

Lois Wyse

Rose's Nut Cups

My mother always thought this recipe was too simple to give to friends, but all of us in the family have at least one piece of my mother's jewelry—and this recipe.

MAKES 24 MINICUPS

9 tablespoons unsalted butter, softened, divided	1 egg, lightly beaten
3 ounces cream cheese, softened	⅔ cup brown sugar
1 cup all-purpose flour	1 teaspoon vanilla extract
	½ cup walnuts, finely chopped

Cream 8 tablespoons butter with cream cheese and add flour. Mix well to form a soft dough. Break dough into small balls (about 24) and press balls down into bottoms and up sides of muffin cups in two 12-cup miniature muffin tins to form shells. Refrigerate for 4 to 6 hours.

Preheat the oven to 325 degrees.

Blend egg, brown sugar, vanilla, and 1 tablespoon butter together. Fill each pastry cup with ½ teaspoon of walnuts, ½ teaspoon of sugar mixture, and top with some chopped nuts. Bake for 25 to 30 minutes.

Allow to cool on a rack.

Apricot Blondies

Adelaide is ninety-five, but that doesn't stop her from baking every day. Her daughter Ethel then picks up Grandma's daily output and delivers it to children and grandchildren. And here's Grandma Adelaide's favorite treat to make.

MAKES 16 PIECES

8 tablespoons unsalted butter
2 cups light-brown sugar, firmly packed
2 large eggs
1½ teaspoons vanilla extract
1¾ cups all-purpose flour, sifted

2 teaspoons baking powder
¼ teaspoon salt
½ cup chopped walnuts
½ cup chopped dried apricots

Preheat the oven to 350 degrees. Grease a 9-inch-square cake pan.

Cream butter with sugar. Add the eggs, vanilla, flour, baking powder, salt, walnuts, and apricots, in order, one at a time, mixing well after each addition. Spread into pan.

Bake 18 to 20 minutes until golden but not overcooked.

For a chewier treat, remove the pan a little earlier. Allow to cool before cutting into squares.

Lois Wyse

You don't have to be Greek to love these moons. Bess's grandmother, who was born in Greece, came to the United States as a child and began making almond moons for Christmas. Now her granddaughter (and namesake) is also making the cookies—which obviously makes her a cookiesake. These cookies melt in your mouth and store well in a cool, dry tin.

MAKES ABOUT 4 DOZEN

½ cup almonds, blanched
2 cups unsalted butter, softened
1 1-pound box confectioners' sugar
2 egg yolks

3 tablespoons cognac
1 teaspoon vanilla extract
3 cups cake flour
½ teaspoon baking powder

Preheat oven to 350 degrees.

Spread almonds on baking sheet and bake until lightly toasted, stirring occasionally, about 10 minutes. Cool and chop finely.

Beat butter with electric mixer on medium-high speed until very light and fluffy, about 6 minutes. Add 3 tablespoons confectioners' sugar, beat 3 minutes. Add egg yolks, cognac, and vanilla and continue beating until smooth. Beat in almonds, flour, and baking powder and mix well. (If dough is very soft, add extra flour, 1 tablespoon at a time.)

Shape dough, one tablespoon at a time, into balls or form into crescents, and place on ungreased cookie sheet.

Bake until very pale golden in color, about 15 minutes. Do not brown. Remove to cooling rack and, while still hot, cover with sifted remaining confectioners' sugar. Roll baked cookies 2 more times at 20-minute intervals.

Chocolate Toffee Squares

When Sherri was growing up, she thought that these toffee squares were just like eating a chocolate bar. Now Sherri's grandchildren are sure it's as good as eating a chocolate bar.

MAKES 24 PIECES

16 tablespoons unsalted butter
1 cup light-brown sugar, firmly packed
1 egg yolk
1 teaspoon vanilla extract
¼ teaspoon salt

2 cups all-purpose flour, sifted
½ pound semisweet chocolate or 12 ounces chocolate chips, melted
1 cup chopped walnuts or pistachio nuts

Preheat oven to 350 degrees. Grease a 9- x 13-inch shallow baking pan.

Cream butter with sugar. Add egg yolk, vanilla, salt, and flour. Mix well. Spread in pan. Bake 20 minutes. Spread on melted chocolate and sprinkle with nuts. Cool completely before cutting into squares.

Lois Wyse

Oatmeal Raisin Crunchies

And how can a dessert section in a cookbook for grandmothers end without a recipe for the best way to fill a cookie jar? Here's our nomination.

MAKES 4 DOZEN CRUNCHIES

8 tablespoons unsalted butter	1½ cups all-purpose flour
½ cup vegetable shortening	1 teaspoon baking soda
1 cup light-brown sugar, firmly packed	1 teaspoon salt
¾ cup sugar	3 cups regular rolled oats
2 large eggs	1 cup chopped pecans or walnuts
1 teaspoon vanilla	1 cup white raisins

Preheat oven to 350 degrees. Have ready 2 ungreased cookie sheets.

Beat butter, shortening, and sugars together until blended. Add eggs and vanilla. Beat until thoroughly mixed. Sift flour with baking soda and salt. Stir oats and sifted flour into butter mixture. Combine well before stirring in nuts and raisins.

Drop spoonfuls of the cookie dough onto cookie sheets. Bake about 15 minutes, until golden.

BRUNCH

WHEN YOU WERE LUCKY ENOUGH TO SLEEP AT GRANDMA'S (BABY-SITTERS ARE A LATTER-DAY INVENTION), SHE NOT ONLY SPOILED YOU WITH more cookies than any parent would allow, she also made the biggest and best breakfasts in memory. Sometimes it was called *brunch*, but to most grandmothers it remained breakfast.

Of course, not all grandmas cook traditional breakfasts for grandchildren. One granddaughter will always remember that her grandmother let her have ice cream for breakfast. Another remembers being allowed to put as much sugar as he wanted on his oat-meal, and a third still remembers how his grandma taught him to make scrambled eggs— just a little water added so the eggs didn't dry out. But the best breakfasts are the ones we chose because Grandma could make anything from muffins and coffee cakes to corn breads and hash. Sometimes the best thing of all was when Grandma made breakfast for dinner, things like blintzes and pancakes.

Oh, those grannies!

Aaaaah, that food!

Brunch

Cheese Blintzes with Hot Fruit Sauce

Puffed Peach Pancake

Hoppel Poppel

Fancy Egg Scramble

Bird in a Hole

Spanish Omelet (Tortilla)

Tarte Grandmere

Banana Bread

Sour-Cream Coffee Cake

Glazed Applesauce Cake

Jonnycakes

Oven French Toast

Spoon Bread

Cheese Blintzes with Hot Fruit Sauce

Margaret's grandmother told her that no girl was old enough to marry until she could make paper-thin, delicate blintzes. In Paris they are known as crêpes, but no matter what your grandmother calls them, everyone agrees that a crêpe (or blintz) can be created only in its special crêpe pan, a pan Grandmother will never wash, nor will we. That pan requires seasoning, and that's part of Granny's secret. Just clean it with a paper towel after each use.

MAKES ABOUT 20 PANCAKES

BLINTZES

1 cup all-purpose flour
dash salt
⅛ teaspoon sugar

1 egg plus 2 yolks
1½ cups milk

Using a mixer or blender, beat all the ingredients together until smooth. Refrigerate batter 30 minutes.

Heat 8-inch skillet over medium heat and rub lightly with butter. (Or melt butter and use a pastry brush to grease pan.) Swirl 2 tablespoons of batter into hot pan. Move pan around to coat batter evenly. Fry, on one side only, until lightly browned. Turn pancake out onto tea towel. Repeat until all the batter has been used. Cool before stacking.

CHEESE FILLING

2 cups dry pot or farmer cheese
2 tablespoons sour cream
4 eggs, lightly beaten

pinch salt
1 tablespoon sugar
grated zest of 1 lemon or orange

Rub pot cheese through fine sieve to remove lumps. Put into bowl and mix with the sour cream, eggs, salt, sugar, and citrus zest.

Lois Wyse

Lay pancake, browned side down, on flat surface. Place a generous spoonful of filling in center. Fold bottom of pancake up and over filling. Fold over sides. Roll to form a small cylinder or envelope.

To serve, heat 1 tablespoon butter in a skillet and gently sizzle pancakes until hot. Serve with fruit sauce.

HOT FRUIT SAUCE

2 tablespoons cornstarch, mixed with 1
   teaspoon water
½ cup sugar
½ cup water

2 cups fresh blueberries or 2 cups pitted
   sour cherries
1 tablespoon fresh lemon juice
grated rind of 1 lemon

Put cornstarch, sugar, and water in a saucepan and whisk well. Stir in fruit and bring to a simmering boil. Stir well. Simmer 5 minutes or until thick and clear. Remove from heat. Stir in rind and juice. Mix well and serve hot over blintzes.

Puffed Peach Pancake

Who ever said Grandmother wasn't a romantic? Here's a charming recipe from our friend Verne for a single pancake for two. Let's call it a lover's breakfast, and admit that our grandmothers had a few good ideas we just might emulate some Sunday morning.

MAKES 2 SERVINGS

3 tablespoons dark-brown sugar, firmly
    packed
⅛ teaspoon cinnamon
1 tablespoon freshly squeezed lemon juice
1 fresh peach, peeled and thinly sliced
2 tablespoons unsalted butter

2 large eggs, lightly beaten
6 tablespoons all-purpose flour
⅛ teaspoon salt
⅓ cup milk
confectioners' sugar, for serving
maple syrup, for serving

Preheat oven to 425 degrees.

Combine I tablespoon brown sugar, cinnamon, and lemon juice. Toss in peach slices.

Divide butter into two 4- x 6- x I-inch ovenproof dishes, and heat dishes in oven to melt butter. Do not brown.

Combine eggs, flour, salt, milk, and remaining brown sugar. Whisk until just combined but still lumpy. Pour batter into baking dishes. Arrange peach slices decoratively on top, reserving marinade. Pour marinade over each.

Bake in center of oven until pancakes are golden and puffed.

Sift confectioners' sugar over top, and serve with maple syrup.

Lois Wyse

Hoppel Poppel

If Sunday is the day you let it all hang out, try hanging out with a little *hoppel poppel*. It is a brunch dish, but Grandma says it makes a mighty fine Sunday night supper, too.

MAKES 4 SERVINGS

4 strips bacon, diced

4 medium potatoes, peeled, cooked, and sliced

3 eggs

3 tablespoons milk

½ teaspoon salt

½ pound cooked ham, cut into small cubes

2 medium tomatoes, peeled and cut into thin wedges

1 tablespoon chopped fresh chives or parsley

In large skillet, cook bacon over medium heat, until transparent. Add potatoes and fry until lightly browned.

In a bowl, blend eggs, milk, and salt. Stir in ham and tomatoes. Pour mixture into skillet and cook until eggs have set. Garnish with chives. Serve immediately.

Fancy Egg Scramble

This is a Grandmother-cleans-the-icebox kind of dish. It's the end of the week, and Granny knows that there are things that just won't keep, so she does what good and thrifty housewives have always done—she makes a brunch version of hash.

MAKES 10 SERVINGS

8 tablespoons butter, divided
½ pound fresh mushrooms, sliced
¼ pound ham, diced
2–3 scallions, chopped
3 tablespoons all-purpose flour
2 cups milk, scalded
salt and freshly ground black pepper to
    taste

1 cup shredded American or mild
    Cheddar cheese
6 eggs, beaten
½ cup dry breadcrumbs
dash paprika

In a skillet, over medium heat, melt I tablespoon butter and sauté mushrooms, ham, and scallions, 2 to 3 minutes, or until golden. Set aside.

In saucepan, over medium heat, melt 3 tablespoons butter until hot and foamy. Stir in flour and cook one minute. Add hot milk slowly, whisking until sauce comes to a boil and thickens. Season with salt and pepper. Mix in mushroom mixture and cheese.

Wipe skillet, and heat 2 tablespoons butter. Add eggs, and cook over low heat until loosely scrambled. Season with salt and pepper and fold into cheese sauce. Pour into 12- x 7- x 2-inch ovenproof glass baking dish.

Over medium heat, heat remaining 2 tablespoons butter in skillet and sauté bread-crumbs and paprika until lightly toasted. Sprinkle over top of dish. Cover and refrigerate until 30 minutes before baking.

Preheat oven to 375 degrees. Bake about 20 minutes, until golden. Serve on buttered toast, if desired.

Lois Wyse

Bird in a Hole

Liza's childhood memories include standing at the stove (she didn't call it a range until much later) and watching her grandmother perform a special magic. Other grandmothers have different names for this dish, but there's never been a grandchild who wasn't fascinated by Grandma's ability to make a hole and drop an egg in it! In fact, this dish is so simple even grandfathers have been known to make it.

MAKES 1 SERVING

1 thick slice firm white bread	*pinch salt*
1 tablespoon butter	*freshly ground black pepper, to taste*
1 large egg	*ketchup*

Spread both sides of bread with butter. Cut out center of slice using a 2½-inch cookie cutter.

In a small skillet, brown bread and cut-out circle lightly on both sides. Remove circle.

Break egg into hole, cover, and cook over gentle heat, until white of egg is firm, about 2 minutes. Transfer to plate and season with salt and pepper. Spread circle with ketchup and place on egg. Serve immediately.

Spanish Omelet

(Tortilla)

We defy anyone to open a refrigerator in a Spanish home and not find a tortilla lurking somewhere between the vegetables and the meat. From the brunch table to the tapas bar, here's the white bread of Spanish cuisine.

1 cup olive oil
1 pound boiling potatoes, peeled and
   sliced ¼" thick

1 medium onion, finely chopped
½ teaspoon salt
6 eggs

Heat oil in 9-inch skillet. Add potatoes and onion. Cover, reduce heat to low, and cook until potatoes are soft, about 25 minutes. Season with salt.

Put eggs in large bowl and beat lightly. Remove potatoes with slotted spoon and fold into egg mixture. Discard all but 2 tablespoons of oil.

Wipe skillet and reheat with reserved oil. Add egg mixture, shaking pan vigorously over medium heat until steam rises around edges, about 10 minutes.

Place large plate or flat lid on pan and invert tortilla onto it. Slide omelet back into pan to cook the other side. Tortilla should be slightly golden.

Turn out onto plate and cut into wedges or 1-inch chunks. Serve at room temperature.

Lois Wyse

Tarte Grandmere

Wouldn't the French grandmother whose recipe we've used be surprised to know that her recipe is in a book? Most of our grandmothers and the grandmothers who preceded them wrote their recipes, if, indeed, they wrote them at all, on scraps of paper that were filed in the "string drawer" of the kitchen. Or they wrote their recipes (sometimes called *receipts*) on file cards and put them in little boxes. Some of us still do. But all of us try to recapture Grandmother's way of making things taste good—even though we may not know exactly how she did it.

MAKES 8 SERVINGS

8 tablespoons butter, softened
3 ounces cream cheese, softened

1¼ cups all-purpose flour
½ teaspoon salt

FILLING

3 large boiling potatoes, peeled, cut into chunks
2 cups small-curd cottage cheese
½ cup sour cream
2 eggs
1 teaspoon salt
freshly ground black pepper, to taste
1 tablespoon chopped fresh parsley
1 teaspoon fresh snipped chives

1 teaspoon fresh snipped dill
2 tablespoons butter
1 small onion, finely chopped
1 pound ham, finely diced
½ cup grated Parmesan cheese

Preheat oven to 400 degrees.

Cream butter and cream cheese with a mixer. Sift flour and salt. Add to mixture, and continue mixing until dough leaves the sides of the bowl and forms into a ball. Wrap and refrigerate at least 30 minutes.

On lightly floured surface, with floured rolling pin, roll dough into a circle to fit 9-inch pie plate. Transfer dough to pie plate. Trim excess. Crimp edges. Line plate with wax

continued on next page

paper. Fill with dried beans, raw rice, or aluminum nuggets. Partially bake crust 10 minutes. Remove wax paper and beans carefully. Reduce oven to 350 degrees.

Cook potatoes until soft. Drain and mash. Add cottage cheese, sour cream, eggs, salt, pepper, parsley, chives, and dill and set aside.

Over medium heat, heat butter in small skillet, and sauté onions and ham to soften, 3 to 5 minutes. Stir into cheese mixture. Spoon into pie shell, sprinkle top with grated Parmesan. Bake until golden brown and puffy, about 45 minutes.

Lois Wyse

Banana Bread

Nobody knows who made the first banana bread, but we'll bet it was the grandmother who saw the three overripe bananas lying on the kitchen counter and murmured, "There must be a way to use these. . . ."

MAKES 10 TO 12 SERVINGS

1 egg

1 cup sugar

8 tablespoons unsalted butter, softened

2 cups all-purpose flour

1 teaspoon baking soda

pinch salt

3 very ripe bananas, mashed well

1 teaspoon vanilla

½ cup walnuts, coarsely chopped, optional

1 tablespoon sugar

½ teaspoon cinnamon

Preheat oven to 350 degrees. Lightly grease a 9- x 5- x 3-inch loaf pan.

Beat egg with sugar until fluffy. Add butter and beat until smooth.

Sift flour with baking soda and salt. Add alternately with bananas and vanilla. Fold in nuts.

Spoon mixture into pan and smooth top. Mix sugar with cinnamon and vanilla. Sprinkle on top. Bake 1 hour, or until top springs back to the touch. Cake should be golden brown.

Cool in pan. Turn onto rack, turn right-side up. Cool completely.

Sour-Cream Coffee Cake

Grandmother liked her coffee hot and strong, and she needed a little sweet to go with it. So, she made a cake that was south of bread, north of dessert—and just right with that ever-present cup of coffee.

MAKES 8 TO 10 SERVINGS

8 tablespoons unsalted butter
¾ cup sugar
1 teaspoon vanilla extract
3 eggs
2 cups all-purpose flour
1 teaspoon baking powder

1 teaspoon baking soda
1 cup sour cream
2 teaspoons cinnamon
1 cup chopped nuts, such as pecans,
　　walnuts, or hazelnuts

Preheat oven to 350 degrees. Grease a 10-inch round baking pan and line bottom with waxed paper.

Cream butter, sugar, and vanilla. Add eggs, one at a time, beating well after each addition. Sift flour with baking powder and baking soda. Add flour, ½ cup at a time, alternating with sour cream, and blend well.

Spread half the batter over bottom of pan. Sprinkle with cinnamon and nuts, and cover with remaining batter. Sprinkle a little more sugar on top.

Bake until lightly browned, 45 to 50 minutes.

Lois Wyse

Glazed Applesauce Cake

Jenny's grandmother made the best applesauce, but even though the family loved it (they praised it outrageously), Grandmother still found she often had applesauce left at the end of the week. So, she made this applesauce cake.

MAKES 16 SQUARES

1 cup dark-brown sugar
½ cup vegetable oil
1½ cups applesauce (see page 153)
2¼ cups flour
2 teaspoons baking soda

1 teaspoon cinnamon
½ teaspoon nutmeg
¼ teaspoon allspice
1 cup white raisins
1 cup walnuts, coarsely chopped

GLAZE

¼ cup dark brown sugar
2 tablespoons unsalted butter

1 tablespoon half-and-half or cream

Preheat oven to 375 degrees. Grease a 9-inch square baking pan.

Beat sugar and oil together in mixer. Beat in applesauce. Sift flour with baking soda, cinnamon, nutmeg, and allspice. Stir flour into applesauce mixture, and mix well. Add raisins and nuts. Spoon batter into baking pan.

Bake until golden brown, 40 to 45 minutes. Cool in pan.

Spread with glaze and cut into squares.

GLAZE:

Combine ingredients together in a small saucepan and bring to a boil. Cook 3 minutes, stirring constantly. Remove from heat. Cover and cool.

Jonnycakes

Jonnycakes were first served in Rhode Island in the early eighteenth century. We don't know if our recipe is the same as the original, but it did come to us from a Newport grandmother who says her family has been serving them ever since she can remember.

MAKES 6 TO 8 SERVINGS

1 cup fine white cornmeal
½ teaspoon salt
2 tablespoons butter, softened
½–1 cup boiling water
¼ cup milk, or as needed

2 tablespoons bacon drippings or
   shortening
melted butter, maple syrup, and/or
   Cheddar cheese, for serving

Using a fork, mix cornmeal, salt, and butter together. Pour in enough boiling water to form a smooth, moist batter, mixing well. There should be no dry lumps and batter should not be wet. Add milk. (Use less milk depending on whether you like a thicker cake or more milk for a more crêpe-like result.)

Heat a skillet or pancake griddle with bacon drippings until very hot. Drop in tablespoons of batter, and reduce heat. Slowly fry cakes, a few at a time, until browned, about 3 to 4 minutes on one side. Cooking time will vary depending on thickness of batter. Cakes should be about 2½ inches in diameter. Keep warm under a towel or napkin until all batter is used.

Serve immediately with melted butter, maple syrup, or grated Cheddar cheese.

Lois Wyse

Oven French Toast

Ruthann remembers that when she and George decided to be married, they had the two families meet for Sunday breakfast. It was Grandma who decided on the menu. "Only one thing is sure to please the two sides," she assured them, "and that's my oven French toast." Grandma was right. The marriage is thirty years old and still going strong.

MAKES 4 SERVINGS

5 large eggs, lightly beaten
1½ cups milk
1 cup cream or half-and-half

1 teaspoon vanilla
½ teaspoon cinnamon
8 slices firm, buttered, white bread

TOPPING

8 tablespoons unsalted butter, softened
1 cup light-brown sugar, firmly packed

2 tablespoons maple syrup or honey
1 cup coarsely chopped pecans

Butter a 9- x 13-inch ovenproof glass baking dish.

Mix eggs, milk, cream, vanilla, and cinnamon. Dip bread slices in egg mixture and place in baking dish. Refrigerate overnight.

Preheat oven to 350 degrees.

Prepare topping. Mix butter, sugar, and syrup in a bowl. Stir in pecans. Spread topping over bread. Bake until golden, about 40 minutes. Serve with preserves or stewed fruit compote.

Spoon Bread

This is a tradition in the South that is slowly but surely working its way north. This is a true grandmother comfort food, a sweet reward for that cold that keeps a grandchild home from school. Of course, you don't have to be a sniffling grandchild to have spoon bread lift your spirits. It works wonders for grown-ups as well.

MAKES 4 TO 6 SERVINGS

2½ cups milk
1 cup white cornmeal
1 teaspoon salt
1 teaspoon sugar

2 tablespoons butter, melted
4 eggs, separated
1 teaspoon baking powder
butter and jam, for serving

Preheat oven to 375 degrees. Butter a 2-quart ovenproof glass baking dish.

In a large saucepan, scald milk. Stir in cornmeal, salt, and sugar. Cook over low heat until thickened, about 5 minutes. Stir in melted butter and set aside. Add egg yolks and baking powder and beat well. Beat whites separately until soft peaks form. Gently fold into cornmeal mixture and spoon into prepared dish.

Bake 30 to 40 minutes until firm and golden. Serve spooned from dish with butter and jam.

Lois Wyse

T E A

FOR GRANDDAUGHTERS WHO LOVE DOLLS, TEA CAN BE AN IMPORTANT CEREMONY. THE TEA PARTY RECALLS A CHARM AND SWEETNESS OF LIFE SO OFTEN MISSING from the angst and anger abroad in the world today. No wonder tea is becoming a more important part of city life.

In re-creating teatime, grandmothers sometimes create an aura that is as important as the baking. Liza remembers her English grandmother as much for tea in the rose garden as for the delicacies that accompanied the tea. There were always jam tarts which Liza helped make by rolling out the pastry and cutting the circles; sultana cake, a raisin quick bread; cherry cake; sponge cake with strawberries and whipped cream (another version of strawberry shortcake); and lots of little no-crust sandwiches spread with butter and thin slices of tomatoes.

Liza's granny is gone now; her roses are faded, but in Liza's kitchen she still lives in her recipes and presides over the tea table of Liza's memory.

Some foods are synonymous with tea.

Doesn't jam go with tea as surely as watercress sandwiches? Even today, there are grandmothers who make their own preserves and marmalades, but none came to her unique recipe in quite the same way as Eason Dobb's grandmother did after she moved to Florida. The year following her move, Grandmother found herself in the midst of one of those September storms that so often batter the Florida coast. After the storm blew through, Grandmother found that every lime, orange, grapefruit, and lemon on her trees had been blown to the ground, filling every inch of her lawn and drive. Being a true grandmother ("Waste not, want not"), she scooped up all the fruit, put sugar on to boil and then invented the marmalade the family now loves. It's called front-yard marmalade. Now Grandmother waits for the September storms; she knows they mean October treats.

All the other tea treats originated in the kitchen of Liza's English grandmother, and this small teatime is dedicated lovingly to her by Liza.

Lois Wyse

Tea

A Perfect Pot of Tea

Russian Tea

Lemon Mint Iced Tea

Orangeade

Scones

Rolled Watercress Sandwiches

Dundee Cake

Scottish Oatcakes

Lemon Poppy-Seed Pound Cake

Shortbread

Front-Yard Marmalade

A Perfect Pot of Tea

Have ready a large porcelain teapot and heat it with a cup of boiling water. Discard water just before adding the tea to be used. In a tea kettle, bring fresh cold water to a full boil. Use good quality loose tea, if possible. Measure one teaspoon of tea per 1 cup of water, plus one teaspoon "for the pot." Put tea in the heated, empty pot and pour in boiling water. Allow to steep five minutes. Serve at once with whole milk or lemon slice and sugar.

Russian Tea

This is a blend of Ceylon and Indian teas; it is black and *very* strong. Serve it in 8-ounce glasses, set in metal holders with handles, with a little dish of cherry preserves on the side. Spoon preserves into tea. Enjoy!

Lemon Mint Iced Tea

Pour 4 cups boiling water over 1 teaspoon chopped fresh mint leaves, strips of lemon peel from one lemon, and 6 tea bags of Orange Pekoe tea. Let steep 10 minutes. Strain and discard mint and tea bags. Stir in simple syrup to taste (about ¼ cup) and the fresh juice of one lemon. Dilute with additional cold water or serve over ice with fresh mint leaves.

SIMPLE SYRUP: Heat 2 cups sugar with 1 cup water until sugar dissolves. Boil 5 minutes. Can be stored indefinitely in the refrigerator.

Orangeade

Remove orange peel from 4 oranges, put into jug, and pour over 2 cups boiling water. Cool. Strain and discard peel. Add strained juice from oranges, ½ cup simple syrup (or to taste), and more water if needed. Serve chilled with or without ice.

Lois Wyse

Scones

2 cups all-purpose flour
1 teaspoon baking powder
pinch of salt
2 tablespoons butter
1 teaspoon sugar

½ cup milk
½ cup currants or white raisins
  (optional)
butter, for serving

Preheat oven to 400 degrees. Grease a cookie sheet.

Sift flour with baking powder and salt. Rub butter into flour mixture. Add sugar. Make a well and stir in just enough milk and raisins, if desired, to form a smooth dough. Turn out on to floured surface and knead with heel of hand. Roll out dough to about ½" in thickness. Cut into rounds or triangles.

Place on cookie sheets and bake until firm when pressed, about 10 to 15 minutes. Split open and butter. Serve immediately.

MAKES 14 SANDWICHES

14 slices enriched sliced white bread
2 3-ounce packages of cream cheese, at
room temperature

1 bunch fresh watercress, trimmed of
thick stems, lightly chopped
salt and freshly ground black pepper to
taste

Trim crusts from bread, and use a rolling pin to gently flatten. Spread each slice with about one tablespoon of cream cheese. Sprinkle with chopped watercress, salt, and pepper. Roll up and place seam-side down on a platter, and cover with a cloth or plastic wrap. Chill well. Rolls may be secured with a toothpick, which should be removed before serving.

VARIATIONS:

These sandwiches can also be made with other fillings, including:

Egg, chicken, and shrimp salad

Smoked salmon with dill (open-faced)

Cucumber and cream cheese

Butter or cream cheese and chives with thin slices of tomato

Grated Cheddar cheese and chutney

Black Forest ham and sweet pickle

Lois Wyse

Dundee Cake

1 cup unsalted butter	½ cup candied cherries
1 cup sugar	2 cups white raisins
4 eggs	½ cup mixed candied peel
1¾ cups all-purpose flour, sifted	grated rind from one lemon
2 cups currants	½ cup almonds, blanched

Preheat oven to 350 degrees. Grease a 9- x 5- x 3-inch loaf pan lined with wax paper.

Cream butter with sugar. Add eggs, one at a time, beating well after each addition. Fold in flour, fruit, peel, rind, and ¼ cup almonds. Pour into baking pan and decorate top with remaining almonds.

Bake until toothpick comes out clean, 1½ to 2 hours. Check occasionally. If almonds start to burn, cover cake lightly with foil. Turn out onto a rack to cool.

Scottish Oatcakes

MAKES 8 OATCAKES

½ cup oatmeal (not instant)
⅛ teaspoon baking soda
⅛ teaspoon salt

1 tablespoon unsalted butter, melted
marmalade or honey, for serving

Preheat oven to 350 degrees. Over high heat, heat a heavy skillet until hot.

Mix oatmeal, baking soda, and salt in a bowl. Make a well. Pour in butter and just enough hot water (about 3 tablespoons) to bind into a firm dough. Sprinkle wooden board with oatmeal, and roll dough out to about ⅛-inch thickness. Cut into 8-inch rounds and again into 8 triangles. Slide onto skillet, smooth side up, and cook until edges begin to curl. Transfer to cookie sheet and bake in oven until toasted but not brown about 5 to 8 minutes.

Lemon Poppy-Seed Pound Cake

2 tablespoons poppy seeds

½ cup milk

1 ¼ cups sugar

½ cup unsalted butter

2 large eggs

1 ¼ cups all-purpose flour

1 teaspoon baking powder

¼ teaspoon salt

1 teaspoon lemon zest

¼ cup fresh lemon juice

Preheat oven to 350 degrees and have ready a 9- x 5- x 3-inch buttered loaf pan. In a small bowl, soak the poppy seeds in the milk. Cream I cup sugar with butter until light and fluffy. Beat in eggs, one at a time.

Sift flour with baking powder and salt. Mix in flour alternately with milk and poppy seeds. Stir in lemon zest. Pour into pan. Bake until toothpick comes out clean when inserted in center, about one hour.

Allow the cake to cool in pan, 5 to 10 minutes. Heat remaining sugar with lemon juice, until dissolved. Using a skewer, poke holes in cake and pour lemon syrup over cake. Let stand 30 minutes or longer, until syrup is absorbed and cake is cool.

Turn out onto platter.

╔═══════════╗
Shortbread
╚═══════════╝

8 tablespoons unsalted butter, softened
¼ cup confectioners' sugar
½ teaspoon vanilla extract (and dash
    almond extract, optional)

1 cup all-purpose flour
¼ teaspoon baking powder
¼ teaspoon salt

Preheat oven to 375 degrees.

Cream butter with sugar. Add vanilla and almond extracts.

Sift flour with baking powder and salt. Stir into butter mixture. Mix until blended into a soft dough.

On a cookie sheet, form the dough into an 8-inch circle. Using the tip of a sharp knife, gently score the top to make 8 to 10 pie wedges. Prick top with tines of a fork and bake until golden, about 20 minutes.

Cut wedges through while shortbread is still warm.

Front-Yard Marmalade

1 grapefruit with peel   2 quarts water
2 oranges with peel   10 cups sugar
2 large lemons with peel

Mince fruit with peel. This may be done with the pulse switch of a food processor. (Cut fruit into chunks first.)

Put fruit in deep pot. Cover with water, bring to a boil, and cook for 10 minutes. Let stand overnight.

Add sugar, and boil mixture again until it reaches 120 degrees on a candy thermometer.* Cool slightly.

Pour into sterile jars through funnel. Cool completely and seal with melted paraffin wax. Store in cool place.

*Mixture should coat the back of a wooden spoon. It is better to undercook than overcook.

TREATS

Making and Baking with Grandmother

PERHAPS ONE OF THE MOST IMPORTANT THINGS A GRANDMOTHER CAN GIVE A GRANDCHILD IS CONFIDENCE IN THE KITCHEN. WATCHING A grandmother lets a child realize that recipes are guides, not mandates. The child observes that a grandmother does the old-fashioned things: She puts a straw in the cake to see if it comes out clean, she makes a crust from scratch, she improvises as she goes along. She finds that what's in the cupboard can substitute for what isn't. And, most important, she finds what's in the heart. The kitchen has a great way of making equals of us all. Anyone can peel a carrot or shell a pea.

And what better fun than sharing the good things we make than with Grandmother? It's a way of bonding, particularly when we don't see one another as often as we'd like; it's a fast way to break the barriers of time and space.

So here's to grannies who cook.

And here's to the children who serve as sous chefs.

Now for some recipes that promise fun in the making, the baking, and, most of all, the eating.

Treats

(Making and baking with Grandmother)

Gingerbread People

Caramel Corn

Baked Jelly Donuts

Caramel Apples

Sugared Pecans and Cashews

Candied Orange and Grapefruit Peel

Cream-Cheese Fudge

Marshmallow Fudge

Rocky Road Candy

Oatmeal Candy

Marble Pudding

Brownies

Peanut Butter and Jelly Cookies

Chocolate Chip Cookies

Hot Chocolate

Gingerbread People

Only "The Nutcracker Suite" can make a child's heart sing the way a gingerbread man can. Now, of course, politically correct grandmothers (like our Grandmother Sherri) insist on making gingerbread *people*. But whatever we call them, children adore them.

MAKES 10 TO 12 THREE-INCH COOKIES

¼ cup unsalted butter
½ cup light-brown sugar
½ cup dark molasses
3½ cups all-purpose flour
1 teaspoon baking soda
½ teaspoon cinnamon
1 teaspoon ginger

¼ teaspoon cloves
¼ teaspoon salt
3–4 tablespoons water
raisins, chocolate or white-chocolate chips, small candies, or bits of dried fruit, tubes of white decorating icing, and so on, for decorating

Preheat oven to 350 degrees. Grease a cookie sheet, gingerbread-man cookie cutter or other shaped cutter. You may also make your own with stiff paper.

Cream butter and sugar together. Beat in molasses.

Sift flour with baking soda, cinnamon, ginger, and cloves. Add sifted flour one-third at a time, alternating each addition with water.

Work mixture into a dough. Roll out, working with the heel of your hands and a rolling pin. Cut dough into shapes and decorate. Bake about 8 minutes or longer. Baking time will vary depending on size and thickness of each cookie. Cookies should spring back slightly when touched. Cool on racks before decorating further with piped icing.

Lois Wyse

Caramel Corn

If you're going to make caramel corn with your grandchild, never leave the kitchen. You're dealing with very hot syrup (so be sure to have the handle on the pot face the back of the range). But here's a fun treat from Jennie, an Idaho granny, to enjoy the next time you watch a movie together.

MAKES 16 CUPS

4 quarts warm freshly popped plain
popcorn
1 cup light brown sugar
1 cup corn syrup
⅓ cup unsalted butter
6 tablespoons evaporated milk

6 tablespoons water
¼ teaspoon baking soda
pinch salt
1 cup salted, skinless peanuts
candy thermometer

Preheat oven to 250 degrees. Grease a cookie sheet.

In a large saucepan, combine sugar, syrup, butter, milk, and water. Cook over medium heat, stirring occasionally, until syrup reaches soft-ball stage (238 degrees). Remove from heat, and stir in baking soda and salt. Pour over popped corn, add peanuts, and stir.

Turn mixture out onto cookie sheet. Bake 20 minutes, stirring occasionally The corn will turn a golden, caramel color, but watch carefully. It should not burn.

Store in airtight container.

Baked Jelly Donuts

Grandma Anne thought that it was a lot of fun to make donuts, but she didn't want the grandchildren to fry them—so she found this recipe for baked donuts and passed it on to us for our grandchildren. Happy dunking!

MAKES 12 DONUTS

1½ cups all-purpose flour
½ cup sugar
2 teaspoons baking powder
¼ teaspoon salt
¼ teaspoon nutmeg
1 large egg

½ cup milk
⅓ cup unsalted butter, melted
½ teaspoon vanilla
5 tablespoons grape jelly, strawberry jam, or orange marmalade

TOPPING:

¼ cup sugar
½ teaspoon cinnamon

3–4 tablespoons butter, melted

Preheat oven to 400 degrees. Butter twelve 2½-inch muffin cups.

Mix flour, sugar, baking powder, salt, and nutmeg. In another bowl, beat egg with milk, butter and vanilla. Stir in flour mixture just to moisten. Spoon half the batter, in equal portions, into muffin cups. Put about 1 teaspoon of jelly in each cup. Spoon on remaining batter to cover.

Bake doughnuts until deep golden, about 18 to 20 minutes. Turn out onto rack.

Mix sugar with cinnamon. Brush donuts with butter and roll in sugar mixture. Serve warm.

Can be stored 1 day in airtight container.

Lois Wyse

Caramel Apples

Even before Halloween became a national holiday to rival Valentine's Day, grandmothers knew that part of the fun of the day was bobbing for apples. But, long ago, grandmothers found that apple pie wasn't the only way to sweeten an apple treat. So have a good time. And remember, making the apples is only the first part. Once made, the children can decorate them.

MAKES 6 CARAMEL APPLES

butter
1 1-pound package vanilla caramels
2 tablespoons water
6 McIntosh apples

6 wooden sticks
garnish: colored sprinkles, chopped nuts,
   or chocolate minichips

Butter a cookie sheet.

Melt caramels and water in top of double boiler over hot but not boiling water. Stir with wooden spoon until smooth. Insert stick into stem end of each apple. Dip into caramel mixture, scrape excess from bottoms, and place on cookie sheet to set, 5 to 10 minutes. Roll in garnish of choice. Chill until firm.

Sugared Pecans and Cashews

Remember how all of us grandmothers always tell our grandchildren we don't want them to buy us something? We'd all rather have something made by the little darlings. Well, here's a little holiday treat Grandma Jo Anne created. Any grandmother will find it especially sweet because it's made by a grandchild!

MAKES 4 CUPS

2 egg whites
1 cup sugar
1 teaspoon cinnamon
1 teaspoon vanilla

½ pound each *roasted whole salted pecans and cashews (or any combination of nuts to equal 1 pound)*
8 tablespoons unsalted butter

Preheat oven to 225 degrees.

In a small bowl, beat egg whites until soft peaks form. Add sugar, cinnamon, and vanilla. Mix well. Pour in nuts.

Melt butter on cookie sheet with 1-inch sides. Pour nut mixture over butter and spread out evenly. Bake 1 to 1¼ hours in upper third of oven, stirring every 15 to 20 minutes. Remove from oven and cool. Store at room temperature in airtight container.

Lois Wyse

Candied Orange and Grapefruit Peel

One of Sue Anne's childhood memories is the tins of candied orange and grapefruit peel that Grandmother always kept in her pantry. And one of the first times Sue Anne slept at Grandmother's, she offered to teach her how to make peel. Sue Anne admits she was so surprised to see Grandmother take real oranges and grapefruits to make the peels. She said, "Somehow I thought candied peels just came candied."

MAKES 3 TO 4 CUPS

3 grapefruits
4–6 oranges or 6–8 lemons

4 cups sugar

Remove the peel and reserve fruit for another use. Slice the peel into narrow strips about 3 inches long. Place strips in a saucepan and cover with cold water, bring to a boil, and boil 2 minutes. Drain and repeat two more times to remove bitter flavor.

Combine equal parts of sugar and water in a large saucepan (4 cups water, 4 cups sugar). Heat to dissolve the sugar while stirring. Add the peel and cook for 1 hour, until translucent. Drain and cool.

Toss in a bowl of granulated sugar. Separate the pieces and allow to dry overnight. Store in an airtight jar.

Cream-Cheese Fudge

Breathes there a child who has never said, "Let's make fudge?" Fudge is as much a part of childhood as grandmothers. So what could be better than one fudge recipe that a grandmother can make with her grandchild? Two fudge recipes, of course—one Liza's, one Sherri's.

MAKES 16 TWO-INCH SQUARES

3 ounces cream cheese	¼ teaspoon vanilla
2 cups confectioners' sugar	dash salt
2 ounces unsweetened chocolate, melted	½ cup chopped walnuts

Butter an 8- x 8-inch-square baking pan.

Beat cream cheese in a bowl. Slowly blend in sugar. Beat until smooth. Add melted chocolate, vanilla, and salt. Stir in nuts. Transfer to pan. Refrigerate at least 20 minutes before cutting into squares.

Marshmallow Fudge

MAKES 64 TWO-INCH SQUARES

4½ cups sugar	1 10-ounce package miniature
1 12-ounce can evaporated milk	marshmallows
3 6-ounce packages chocolate chips	1 teaspoon vanilla
1½ cups unsalted butter	2 cups chopped nuts

In a large saucepan, mix sugar and milk over medium heat. Slowly bring mixture to a rolling boil. Boil 8 minutes. Remove from heat and stir in chocolate chips and butter. Continue mixing until mixture has melted. Blend in marshmallows, vanilla, and nuts.

Spread in 9- x 13- x 2-inch ungreased baking pan. Cool before cutting into squares.

Lois Wyse

Rocky Road Candy

Here's a candy as easy to make as the cereal-based candies, but we think it has a contemporary twist with the addition of sunflower seeds. It comes from Steven, a grandchild in Florida.

MAKES 32 TWO-INCH SQUARES

2 cups chocolate chips	½ cup nuts, coarsely chopped
2¼ cups miniature marshmallows	¼ cup sunflower seeds

Have ready foil-lined 8-inch-square baking pan.

Melt chocolate chips in the top of a double boiler until smooth. Remove from heat and stir in remaining ingredients. Spread in pan and chill until firm. Remove foil from pan and peel away from candy. Cut into squares.

Oatmeal Candy

ext time a grandchild won't eat his oatmeal, try this little recipe from Barbara, a Chicago grandmother who passed it along to us.

MAKES ABOUT 24 DROPS

2 cups sugar
8 tablespoons unsalted butter
¼ cup milk
dash salt
4 tablespoons cocoa

3 cups uncooked rolled oats (not instant)
1 teaspoon vanilla
½ cup shredded coconut and/or peanut butter (optional)

Have ready a cookie sheet lined with wax paper.

In a saucepan, heat sugar, butter, milk, salt, and cocoa. Do not boil. Stir in oatmeal and vanilla. Add coconut and peanut butter, if desired. Stir and drop onto cookie sheet a teaspoonful at a time, to cool.

Lois Wyse

Marble Pudding

Sherri's mother, Esther, made this for years, and she put the surprise vanilla wafer in the bottom. "I still make her recipe, and my grandchildren look forward to the surprise just as much as I did when I was a child," Sherri recalls.

MAKES 8 SERVINGS

VANILLA PUDDING

4 tablespoons sugar
3 tablespoons cornstarch
dash salt

2 cups milk
1 teaspoon vanilla

CHOCOLATE PUDDING

6 tablespoons sugar
3 tablespoons cornstarch
dash salt
2 ounces unsweetened chocolate,
    chopped, or ⅓ cup Dutch-process
    cocoa

2 cups milk
1 teaspoon vanilla
2–3 ripe bananas, sliced
6 vanilla wafers

Have ready 8 1-cup individual glass bowls.

continued on next page

PREPARE THE VANILLA PUDDING:

Put sugar, cornstarch, and salt into a saucepan. Stir in milk, over medium heat. Continue stirring until mixture thickens. Add vanilla. Continue cooking gently 2 to 3 minutes more.

PREPARE THE CHOCOLATE PUDDING:

Put sugar, cornstarch, and salt into a saucepan. Combine chocolate with milk and add to the pan. Cook over medium heat until chocolate has melted and pudding is smooth and thick. Add vanilla and continue cooking 2–3 minutes.

Put vanilla wafer and 2 to 3 slices of banana into the bottom of each bowl. Spoon in pudding, alternating chocolate and vanilla. Swirl the pudding once with a knife to create a marbled effect.

Cover with plastic wrap and chill well before serving.

Lois Wyse

Brownies

If you have never made brownies with a child, then maybe you're not a mother or a grand-mother. Brownies are everyone's first dessert, everyone's first recipe, and everyone's life-time favorite. Eat them plain. Drown them in chocolate syrup. Top them with ice cream. Doesn't matter. Nothing can hurt a brownie. This recipe came from a grandmother in Prov-idence.

MAKES 16 TWO-INCH SQUARES

1 cup unsalted butter

4 ounces unsweetened chocolate

2 cups sugar

1 teaspoon vanilla extract

4 eggs, lightly beaten

1 ¼ cups sifted all-purpose flour

½ teaspoon salt

½ cup chopped walnuts or ½ cup
     chocolate chips may be added to the
     batter before baking

confectioners' sugar, for serving

Preheat oven to 400 degrees. Butter and flour a 9-inch-square baking pan.

Melt butter and chocolate in top of double boiler until smooth. Set aside to cool, 5 min-utes.

Stir sugar and vanilla into chocolate, add eggs, and mix well. Stir in flour and salt with wooden spoon. Mix until all ingredients are *just* combined. Do not overmix.

Spread batter into prepared pan and bake exactly 18 minutes, to keep brownies "fudgy." Cool in pan and cut into squares. Sprinkle with confectioners' sugar before serv-ing.

Peanut Butter and Jelly Cookies

You can be sure that no grandmother brought this recipe with her on the Mayflower. This isn't one of those old-time recipes with its roots in Europe or any other part of the world. Peanut butter and jelly is just sort of nouveau American, but it's so darned good that a lot of us keep eating the combination all our lives. Liza and Sherri created this cookie recipe because they figured that you just can't get enough peanut butter.

MAKES ABOUT 2 DOZEN COOKIES

4 tablespoons vegetable shortening
4 tablespoons unsalted butter
½ cup smooth peanut butter
½ cup sugar
½ cup light-brown sugar
1 egg
2 tablespoons milk

1 teaspoon vanilla extract
2 cups all-purpose flour
1 teaspoon baking soda
½ teaspoon salt
grape or strawberry jam
    and extra peanut butter,
    to finish

Preheat oven to 375 degrees. Have ready a cookie sheet.

Cream shortening, butter, and peanut butter together with the sugars. Beat in egg, milk, and vanilla.

Sift flour with baking soda and salt. Add to egg mixture and continue mixing until thoroughly combined.

Pinch off teaspoons of dough, roll into balls, and place on cookie sheet. Flatten slightly with fork. Bake until lightly browned, 10 to 12 minutes. Allow cookies to cool before spreading with peanut butter and jelly. Top with another cookie to make "sandwiches."

Lois Wyse

Chocolate Chip Cookies

Grandkids love to eat chocolate chip cookies. Or so we thought until we heard about the little boy who said to his grandmother, "Well, okay, I'll bake with you if I have to, but don't make me eat the cookies. Just let me eat the batter." But we still think that most grand-children will love to eat the still-warm cookies they've made with a big glass of milk. What a way to end a day!

MAKES ABOUT 6 DOZEN COOKIES

8 tablespoons unsalted butter, at room
   temperature
1 cup light brown sugar, firmly packed
1 egg
½ teaspoon vanilla extract
1⅛ cups all-purpose flour
½ teaspoon baking soda
¼ teaspoon salt

6 ounces bittersweet
   chocolate, preferably
   Swiss, broken into
   pieces
½ cup chopped pecans or
   filberts (optional)
½ teaspoon powdered instant
   coffee (optional)

Preheat oven to 375 degrees. Grease a baking sheet.

Cream butter with sugar. Beat in egg and vanilla. Sift flour with baking soda and salt. Beat in sifted flour. Stir in chocolate pieces, nuts, and instant coffee. Drop teaspoons of dough onto cookie sheet and bake 8 minutes or until golden.

Remove cookies with a metal spatula. Allow to cool on wire rack.

Hot Chocolate

All the world over, grandchildren have memories of Granny's serving hot chocolate as a going-to-bed ritual. Megan, who grew up in England, however, recalls hot chocolate with her grandmother for "elevenses," an II A.M. treat. In Copenhagen, Nellie was picked up from school by her grandmother, and the two walked home together. The delight of getting home was to have Grandmother make her a big cup of hot chocolate with lots and lots of whipped cream. What was it we all loved so much—was it the chocolate or was it the mounds of that rich, buttery cream that cooled the hot chocolate?

MAKES 2 SERVINGS

| 2 cups whole milk | 2 tablespoons sugar |
| 2 tablespoons Dutch-process cocoa | ½ cup whipped cream |

In a small saucepan, heat milk, stir in cocoa and sugar. Continue heating, stirring constantly, until cocoa and sugar have dissolved. Pour into mugs, spoon on whipped cream and a little dusting of cocoa.

Lois Wyse

INDEX